2/98

D0194136

At
the Essence
of Learning:
Multicultural Education

1992–94 Kappa Delta Pi Biennial

At the Essence of Learning: Multicultural Education is the culmination of the Society's two-year study of issues and practices related to the biennial theme of "Celebrating Diversity." This biennial is the first of many books that the Society will commission each biennium to explore critical issues in education in ways that develop new knowledge and new understandings.

The primary mission of Kappa Delta Pi, an International Honor Society founded in 1911, is to recognize and reward excellence in education.

At the Essence of Learning: Multicultural Education

Geneva Gay
University of Washington—Seattle

Kappa Delta Pi, an International Honor Society in Education
West Lafayette, Indiana
1994

Copyright © 1994 by Kappa Delta Pi,
an International Honor Society in Education

All rights reserved. No part of the material protected by this copyright notice
may be reproduced or utilized in any form or by any means, electronic or mechanical, including photocopying,
recording, or by any information storage and retrieval system, without the permission of the publisher.

Direct all inquiries to the Director of Publications,
Kappa Delta Pi, P.O. Box A, West Lafayette, Indiana 47906-0576.

Project Editors:	Carol Bloom
	Leslie Rebhorn
Editorial Assistants:	Jill Jones
	Linda Heaton
Text and Cover Design:	Angela Bruntlett
Cover Illustration:	Michel Tcherevkoff/The Image Bank Chicago

Library of Congress Cataloging-in-Publication Data

Gay, Geneva
    At the essence of learning: multicultural education/Geneva Gay. 1st ed.
    p. cm.

    Includes bibliographical references and Index.
    ISBN 0-912099-14-3

    1. Multicultural education—United States—Philosophy. I. Title.
    LC1099.3.G39 1994

    370.19'6—dc20   94-13977
                                                        CIP

Printed in the United States of America

94   95   96   97   98   5   4   3   2   1

Call Kappa Delta Pi International Headquarters (800-284-3167) to order.
Quantity discounts for more than 20 copies.   KDP Order Code 501

370.196
GAY
1996

Author

Geneva Gay is Professor of Education at the University of Washington—Seattle, where she teaches courses in general curriculum theory and multicultural education. Professor Gay is also an Associate of the Center for Multicultural Education. She is the author of 90 articles and book chapters, and is the co-editor of *Expressively Black: The Cultural Basis of Ethnic Identity* (Praeger, 1987). She is also an internationally known consultant on cultural diversity in teacher education, curriculum development, staff development, and classroom instruction. Dr. Gay received the Multicultural Educator Award in 1994, the first given by the National Association of Multicultural Education.

Dedication

For
Juston and Jason
*Symbols of the message, spirit, vision, and hope
embodied herein*

CONTENTS

Acknowledgments

To Rosa, without your boundless energy, I could never have completed this document on time. I am forever indebted to you.

To all of the unnamed students and teachers who, unknowingly, provided me with the inspiration to write this book with the hope that it will contribute, in some small way, to making their journey toward educational excellence somewhat easier.

To George L. Mehaffy and Kappa Delta Pi for the invitation and opportunity to undertake this project.

Preface

For the 1992–94 biennium, Kappa Delta Pi selected "Celebrating Diversity" as its theme to focus attention on one of the crucial issues of our day. How will the United States and other countries address the diversity of people and ideas found within national borders? While diversity has always been present, it has often been ignored or repressed. At the threshold of the twenty-first century, however, no one can ignore the growing diversity of cultures, ethnicities, and languages, as well as the diversity of ideas and values, found in our increasingly global village.

The question for Kappa Delta Pi members, as well as for educators everywhere, is how we will respond. How will Kappa Delta Pi members, as educators, take advantage of the opportunities that diversity presents? As we began the biennium, I urged Kappa Delta Pi to consider issues of diversity, particularly as played out in schools. Since then, a remarkable number of activities have focused on the theme: regional conferences have invited speakers and encouraged discussions; our two journals have provided substantial scholarly attention to the topic; individual KDP chapters have developed rich and interesting programs; and our 1994 convocation in Orlando offers a powerful collection of workshops and presentations. Numerous and varied activities throughout our society attest to our commitment as teachers and learners to continue our own intellectual journeys. It has indeed been a celebration.

Of all the challenges facing schools today, the greatest challenge remains the central one: how to ensure success for all children. Our special challenge, as Kappa Delta Pi members and teachers, is to create educational opportunities for all children. The first ideal of Kappa Delta Pi, affirmed upon becoming a member, is the pledge of Fidelity to Humanity. We have dedicated ourselves to the proposition that "through continuous education, based on equal opportunity, persons of all ages, races, and creeds shall find increased opportunity for experiencing more meaningful lives." This book by Professor Geneva Gay was written with that ideal in mind.

For the past decade, since the publication of *A Nation at Risk* in 1983, school reform has been a major political and educational issue in the United States. There is a popular perception that schools are failing and that a variety of increasingly radical plans must be adopted to prevent further erosion of excellence. I find the public dialogue about school failure curious, since it often seeks "remedies" such as charter schools, voucher initiates, shared decision making, and site-based governance. These issues, it seems to me, describe the distribution of power rather than the education of children. In my opinion, schools in the United States are not failing universally. After all, the public school system in the United States has been at least partly responsible for our global leadership in science and technology, our premier position in Nobel Prize recipients, and our universally recognized system of higher education. Public schools cannot be complete failures if they still allow this country to enjoy its many leadership roles. To condemn public schools universally is to scapegoat teachers, blaming them for a society's failures. Furthermore, the condemnation of all schools prohibits thoughtful analysis, masking the real issues. Schools have not failed universally; they have, instead, failed differentially—for some children and in some neighborhoods. That is an important insight, for the acknowledgment of this problem is the first step in making schools better for children.

Geneva Gay begins with a simple premise: good teaching and multicultural teaching are indistinguishable. Her book takes us on an odyssey, an exploration of the ideas and concepts embedded in the term "multicultural education." She appropriately reviews the political controversy that has shaped the dialogue about multicultural education from its inception. Multiculturalism has become, like so many issues in education, a political argument, a controversy not only of philosophies but a struggle between those whom the system serves and those whom it does not. But beyond the rhetoric and confrontation, multi-culturalism is also a battle about competing visions of the United States and the world.

Dr. Gay writes this book for teachers rather than rhetoricians and politicians. Her effort is to demystify multicultural education, removing it from the political arena and locating it in the educational arena. Once it is placed in an educational context, multiculturalism can be evaluated for its impact and success in achieving our often-stated and common goals for children. In Dr. Gay's view, multicultural education is not a fringe or radical movement designed to threaten the basic underpin-nings of life in the United States. Instead, she affirms its place in the mainstream of American educational thought and practice. Like the early-twentieth-century writings of John Dewey and current successful school practices, Dr. Gay reminds us that the child is the meaning-maker, and that our task as teachers is to build structures and create strategies that help all children gather meaning from their surroundings. She argues that multicultural education considers the child's back-ground, prior knowledge, and areas of interest and experience, an approach that has been labeled "progressive education" since the beginning of this century.

The celebration of diversity is accompanied by a curious paradox: the more we focus on and celebrate our differences, the more we recognize our similarities. Geneva Gay's book reminded me that, as Kappa Delta Pi members, educators, and human beings, we share substantial common views about education and the future. We have, in our KDP creed and in the Declaration of Independence and Constitu-tion of the United States, declared a shared set of core values about the human experience, joined together in hopes for a better future, and expressed our common aspirations for our children. Celebrating our diversity becomes, paradoxically, a means for bringing us together, not dividing us.

A number of people deserve credit for this very important undertaking. The Executive Council of Kappa Delta Pi authorized this project as a commitment to our members and the ideals we share. Carol Bloom and her publications department staff at Kappa Delta Pi headquarters deserve special recognition for the long hours they devoted to this effort. Special thanks go to the manuscript reviewers—H. Prentice Baptiste of the University of Houston; Wanda S. Fox of Purdue University; Joyce E. King of Santa Clara University; Kent Koppelman of the University of Wisconsin—LaCrosse; and Ellen Shiflet of Starbuck Middle School in Racine, Wisconsin—whose perceptive comments added to this volume. But most of all, I want to thank Geneva Gay, whose substantial contributions to the field of education through the years are reflected in this book. Her most important message is a reminder to us all. In another era, teachers took pride in saying that they treated all children alike; today that would be more of an indictment than a source of pride. Not all children can be treated alike, for children come from different backgrounds, different experiences. If they are to become meaning-makers, we must provide them with equality of opportunity rather than equality of treatment. Equality of opportunity includes recognizing differences and treating children as unique and special human beings with unique and special needs. To achieve our goals as a society that honors education—and children—we can do no less.

George L. Mehaffy
President of Kappa Delta Pi
1992–94

Introduction

Dear Readers:

Welcome to what I hope will be an exciting, engaging, and enlightening dialogue. Multicultural education and cultural diversity are critical, controversial, and increasingly unavoidable issues in our society and schools. As we advocate and design educational programs and practices that are more effective for greater numbers of culturally diverse students, thus building a more inclusive, egalitarian, and just society, we need to understand how multicultural education and general education are related. Some individuals claim that these two are irreconcilable opposites; others suggest that they are highly complementary. An examination of the key underlying principles of both is one way to begin to resolve this conflict. This is the major purpose of *At the Essence of Learning*.

The intent, vision, and spirit that underlie the text of this book were articulated by one of my favorite authors, Maya Angelou (1993, 124). She noted:

> It is time for the preachers, the rabbis, the priests and
> pundits, and the professors to believe in the awesome
> wonder of diversity so that they can teach those who follow
> them. It is time for parents to teach young people early on
> that in diversity there is beauty and there is strength. We
> all should know that diversity makes for a rich tapestry,
> and we must understand that all the threads of the
> tapestry are equal in value no matter their color; equal in
> importance no matter their texture.

The rapidly increasing diversity in U.S. society and schools along ethnic, racial, cultural, and social lines is causing much discussion, debate, and controversy. New immigrants from Southeast Asia, the Middle East, Africa, Central and South America, and eastern Europe add even more diverse languages, values, cultures, and experiences to those that already exist in the United States. All segments of society—government, business, law, religion, media, and education—are concerned about the kinds of adaptations needed to accommodate cultural and ethnic pluralism in their respective areas of influence. An additional factor of particular concern to educators is the high percentage of academic failure among students from some of these groups. Included in this category are children who are poor, live in large urban centers, have limited English proficiency, or are from groups of color such as African-Americans, Puerto Rican-Americans, Mexican-Americans, Native Americans, and some Asian-Americans. As the elements of cultural pluralism increase in society, so does the challenge of negotiating it in schools, places of worship, businesses, courts, and governments.

Conscientious educators are asking themselves: What should we do about ethnic, linguistic, and cultural pluralism in the classroom? How do we reconcile it with education's commitment to perpetuating a common national culture? Some suggest that the answers to these questions can be found in multicultural education—a way of thinking and acting in the classroom that accepts the cultural differences of students from various ethnic, racial, and social groups as valuable attributes to be included in educational programs and practices. Other educators view multicultural education as contradicting the vision of the United States as one nation, indivisible. This vision is commonly conveyed as *e pluribus unum*—making one cohesive culture and unified nation out of all of the different peoples and influences that comprise the United States.

This book takes the position that national identity and cultural pluralism, general education and multicultural education, *pluribus* and *unum* are not inherently contradictory or incompatible; they are complementary and reciprocal. These relationships can be discerned by analyzing the major social values and related principles fundamental to the goals, programs, and practices of the educational process.

The primary focus of analysis here is on the similarity between principles of general education and of multicultural education, not the definitions or implementation of these processes, per se. Numerous statements about what these two sets of principles are exist elsewhere, and they are easily retrievable from professional textbooks, journal articles, and policy documents; therefore, they are not discussed in any of the chapters. However, it may be useful for you to have some idea of my definitions since they do significantly influence the discussions about educational principles developed in this book.

I define multicultural education as *the policies, programs, and practices employed in schools to celebrate cultural diversity. It builds on the assumption that teaching and learning are invariably cultural processes. Since schools are composed of students and teachers from a wide variety of cultural backgrounds, the best way for the educational process to be most effective for the greatest number of students is for it to be multicultural.* As used in this definition, *to celebrate* means to know, believe, accept, value, use, and promote cultural diversity as a normal feature of humankind, a characteristic trait of U.S. society, and an essential component of quality education for *all* students. Effective implementation of multicultural education requires a combination of the personal attitudes and values of educators, curriculum content, instructional methods and materials, classroom climates and the participation of individuals at all levels of the educational enterprise.

Nieto (1992) provided a detailed *descriptive* definition of multicultural education that is an excellent complement to and extension of my own, but much more specific and encompassing of the major substantive dimensions endorsed by most advocates and addressed in this book. According to Nieto (1992, 208), multicultural education is:

> *a process of comprehensive school reform and basic education for all students. It challenges and rejects racism and other forms of discrimination in schools and society and accepts and affirms the pluralism (ethnic, racial, linguistic, religious, economic, and gender, among others) that students, their communities, and teachers represent. Multicultural education permeates the curriculum and instructional strategies used in schools, the interactions among teachers, students, and parents, and the very way that schools conceptualize the nature of teaching and learning. Because it uses critical pedagogy as its underlying philosophy and focuses on knowledge, reflection, and action (praxis) as the basis for social change, multicultural education furthers the democratic principles of social justice.*

Embedded in Nieto's (1992) definition are seven key characteristics of multicultural education:

> *in opposition to all forms of oppression; fundamental to educational excellence and equality; for all students in all school settings; comprehensive and pervasive across the total educational enterprise; devoted to promoting social justice; inclusive of both curriculum content and instructional processes; and committed to teaching critical analysis and self-reflection in all learning.*

I agree with Miller and Seller (1985) that education has three major functions, and I think that these should be addressed in concert with each other. These functions are *transmission, transaction,* and *transformation.* The *transmissive* function of education involves passing on to students the cultural heritages of all peoples and teaching them the basic skills needed to perform the various roles they will play as adult members of society—citizen, parent, worker, consumer. Education that is *transactive* recognizes that students as well as teachers are key players in teaching-learning interactions. Both, along with their contributions, experiences, and perspectives, should be actively engaged in determining how the educational process unfolds. Furthermore, schools and education programs have the obligation not only to teach students facts about their cultural heritages and how to understand existing conditions, but also how to envision and create a better future for themselves and society. That is, students need to know how to *transform* present personal and social boundaries in order to improve the quality of life for all individuals, groups, and societies.

Educational principles are commonly accepted beliefs about the purposes and processes of teaching and learning. They reflect the cultural values of the societies in which schools exist. For example, most educators in the United States accept without question the belief that if something is of personal significance to students, they will learn it more easily than that which is not. Most educators also accept that schools are obligated to serve the needs of individual students as well as society. Consequently, education in the United States will be quite different from that in China or Nigeria because the three societies are quite different. And, the education of all students within the United States will be similar because of the country's shared culture, but unique because of individual traits, ethnic orientations, and cultural heritages.

The key questions that guide discussion throughout this book are (1) What is the relationship between principles of general and multicultural education? and (2) Why is it important for teachers to understand this relationship? *At the Essence of Learning* explores how beliefs about multicultural education are, in effect, restatements or translations of general education principles. Its primary focus on clarifying this philosophical relationship is based on the assumption that teaching behaviors are grounded by values and beliefs. Therefore, if educators are to be effective in changing their instructional, curricular, and policy practices related to cultural diversity and multicultural education, they must revise the values and beliefs that undergird them. This knowledge helps to ensure that the highest quality educational opportunities and outcomes are available to the full range of students who populate our schools. It also aids in revising instructional practices to ensure they are compatible with societal developments.

The discussions throughout this book are not intended to teach you how to teach multicultural education in the classroom. Rather, they concentrate on improving the understanding of multicultural education as a set of values, beliefs, and ideas about how to make schooling more effective and meaningful to a greater number and variety of students. They clarify some of the misconceptions that surround multicultural education and demonstrate how it fits into the broader context of U.S. values and visions about social and political democracy, as well as educational quality, equity, and excellence for all students. Of course, all of these discussions have direct and profound implications for instructional practice, but they are more often implied than stated explicitly. This book is directed more toward clarifying the *values* and *visions* of multicultural education than explaining its *content* and *methods*. Consequently, *At the Essence of Learning* is not a typical teaching methods textbook.

Inevitably, teachers have to explain, and often defend, the reasons for their classroom practices and priorities. This is particularly so when the issues in question are controversial. As we will see, multicultural education is very controversial. The major parameters and points of this controversy are explored in this book. The insights gained from these examinations will improve your overall understanding of the nature and intent of multicultural education, as well as prepare you to explain your opinions about why and how cultural pluralism should be included in school programs, policies, and practices.

Chapter 1 examines some of the commonly accepted principles of general education and some of the conflicting conceptions of multicultural education. The principles discussed are organized within the categories of human growth and development, socialization and citizenship, and teaching and learning. These categories establish the conceptual baseline for Chapters 3 through 5.

The focus of discussion in Chapter 2 is the debate over multicultural education and the major principles associated with teaching for and about cultural diversity. The main areas and voices of the debate are identified, and the key contentions of both critics and advocates are summarized. These explorations should facilitate your understanding of why critics feel that multicultural education contradicts general education and why advocates feel that it is complementary. The ideas generated by this debate establish the parameters for subsequent discussions of specific beliefs about teaching and learning in a multicultural society like the United States. Thus, Chapters 1 and 2 serve as an overview for Chapters 3 through 5.

Each of the remaining chapters develops in detail a different set of general and multicultural education principles. Chapter 3 focuses on principles dealing with human growth and development and their implications for general and multicultural education. Principles of education related to developing skills for democratic citizenship are examined in Chapter 4. The discussion in Chapter 5 is devoted to principles of pedagogy—that is, beliefs regarding the most effective methods of teaching and learning.

All chapters conclude with a short section entitled "Reflections and Applications." The Reflections encapsulate the main messages of the chapter in a few summary statements. The Applications suggest activities for the reader to explore as a means of further clarifying and crystallizing the ideas discussed in the narrative text of the chapter.

Two features recur across the application activities. First, they include suggestions for what readers can do to further extend their personal understanding of the ideas, issues, and messages discussed in the chapter. Second, there are also suggested activities that readers who are teachers might do with their students and/or colleagues to improve their understanding of and competency in multiculturalism. Frequently, the Applications provide opportunities for you to track the growth of your own increasing understanding of multicultural education. Some application activities suggest that you begin an activity before reading or within the first few pages of a chapter. Then return to the same activity after reading the chapter, and compare your attitudes, understanding, and/or actions on some aspect of multicultural education. The underlying assumption is that you will learn from reading the chapters. But, this is only the beginning of the learning process. The end-of-chapter Applications provide additional and varied opportunities to continue the learning that begins with reading the narrative text.

I included the combination of application activities for several reasons: the importance of reflection and introspection in the professional development of teachers; the interrelationship among values, beliefs, attitudes, and actions in teaching and learning; the empowering potential of knowledge; and the nature of effective implementation of multicultural education as a multidimensional process. Educators must *act* in many different ways and on many different fronts simultaneously to "do" multicultural education well. Therefore, the suggested Applications invite you to explore yourself; to practice translating knowledge into actions; to become actively engaged in the professional development of colleagues around issues of multicultural education and cultural pluralism; and, on occasion, to translate the insights you gain about multicultural education into instruction for students.

The recurrent message across all discussions in all chapters of this book is that the meaning and intent of principles of general education and multicultural education are essentially the same. They differ only in context, operational details, and constituent groups. Principles of general education function at a global, universal level, and apply to all students. By comparison, those of multicultural education place general ideas about teaching and learning into the context of different racial, ethnic, and social groups, cultures, and experiences. They validate the perspectives and frames of reference of students who are poor, from groups of color, female, immigrant, or whose first language is not English, along with those of the middle-class, European-American dominant groups in our society.

The book concludes with a short Epilogue. It summarizes and underscores two key ideas that were developed in the preceding chapters: (1) Multicultural education is an embodiment of our nation's commitment to the democratic values of freedom, equality, and justice for all citizens; and (2) Multicultural education is inextricably interrelated with the vision of educational excellence for all students.

You are invited to be an active participant in the dialogues about the different dimensions of the complementary and reciprocal relationships between principles of multicultural and general education that take place in this book. As you read the chapters, compare the explanations and interpretations provided with your own perceptions and thoughts. Extend the examples offered to incorporate your own personal experiences. Sometimes this may entail replacing the examples provided with your own. Do not hesitate to do so. When questions are suggested as invitations for you to engage with the ideas, accept the challenge wholeheartedly and "think along" with the author in search of answers and explanations. Try out the suggested activities in your own professional arena to see if they work for you. Encourage your colleagues and students to interact with you in dialogues around the issues discussed in this book. Continually remind yourself, your students, and your colleagues that multicultural education is for all students, subjects, times, and settings, not just for students of color, social studies and language arts, or when racial tensions among students occur in schools.

This kind of active and continuous engagement will make the ideas presented herein a "personal encounter" for you rather than merely an abstract, dispassionate reading of the author's ideas and arguments. Education should always be a passionate and personal involvement. As Taba (1962, 151) suggested, "Vital learning is experiencing of a sort" that engages the mind and emotions simultaneously by integrating important knowledge, profound feeling, and thoughtful reflection. It causes us to "feel what we know and to know what we feel" (Moholy-Nagy 1947, 11). *At the Essence of Learning* should be such an experience for you. It should also be affirming and informing.

If, after you have completed reading this book, you have a better understanding of the fallacies of contentions that multicultural education is inconsistent or is in competition with the values of general education, then I have succeeded in achieving my purpose. You will have begun to establish a powerful foundation for pursuing instructional actions that incorporate multiculturalism in all dimensions of the educational enterprise. You will also have begun to model the conviction that for education to serve its social and personal development functions for all citizens of the United States, it must, of necessity, be culturally pluralistic. You will be well on the way to truly understanding that multicultural education is, indeed, the essence of all quality learning for the ethnically, culturally, socially, and racially diverse students who populate our schools.

I hope that participating in this dialogue is a memorable occasion for you, one that you will return to often throughout your professional career, and one that you will entice others to join.

Geneva Gay

Geneva Gay
University of Washington—Seattle
March 1994

References

Angelou, M. 1993. *Wouldn't take nothing for my journey now*. New York: Random House.

Miller, J., and W. Seller. 1985. *Curriculum perspectives and practice*. New York: Longman.

Moholy-Nagy, L. 1947. *Vision in motion*. Chicago: Paul Theobald.

Nieto, S. 1992. *Affirming diversity: The sociopolitical context of multicultural education*. New York: Longman.

Taba, H. 1962. *Curriculum development: Theory and practice*. New York: Harcourt, Brace and World.

Chapter 1

Principles of General Education

Our society has developed the belief that schooling is a way of transmitting and conserving, expanding and rectifying the knowledge, values, and skills antecedent to a life of purpose, of work, of accomplishment, of personal growth. . . . Schools were invented, organized, and developed to serve as agents of society . . . to inculcate in the young habits of good choice which were meant to sustain visions of excellence, of greatness, and of the power of knowledge and high conduct.

(Brandwein 1981, 3)

Creating schools in which all the nation's children receive a high-quality education will not be easy. But behind every significant achievement are dreamers and visionaries. . . . We must have a vision, but we must also have the will to act. Forging that will is perhaps our greatest challenge.

(Banks 1993, 48)

What are the underlying values of educational practices characteristic of American schools? What deeper beliefs do they symbolize? Why do we have students engage in competitive learning activities, pledge allegiance to the flag, raise their hands before speaking out in class, study certain subjects, and celebrate particular holidays? Do you ever analyze your own reasons for making particular instructional decisions to determine the values and beliefs that generated them? A decision to teach students facts before they engage in critical thinking, algebra before geometry, or sentence structure before writing compositions may reflect a certain belief about the sequence of learning. It may be that learning is a developmental process that moves from simple and concrete experiences to more complex and abstract ideas. Teaching students about different cultural groups and heritages in the United States before studying world cultures may be driven by a similar belief. The results of these explorations about how teaching and learning occur, and to what ends, comprise the content of educational principles.

The discussion of the principles of general education in this chapter follows a fourfold structure. The discussion begins with a brief definition of principles and an explanation of their function in the educational process. A description of the process used to identify and classify principles of general education follows. The principles are grouped into three categories: *human growth and development, citizenship and socialization,* and *teaching and learning.* The chapter concludes with some suggestions for reflecting on and applying the implications for practice embedded in the principles. The principles of general education themselves are discussed in more detail in Chapters 3 through 5.

Role of Principles

Educational principles are statements of beliefs and ideals about the purpose, content, nature, and function of teaching and learning. They create philosophical visions and ethical standards by which to design and assess instructional plans and actions. Principles of general education in the United States are "generic" ideas about teaching and learning. As such, they do not refer to any specific group or individual; instead, they are assumed to apply to everyone. One example of a principle is:

> *the active participation of students in the learning process leads to greater depth of understanding, easier task mastery, and more persistence and transfer of learning.*

Before continuing to read this chapter, complete Chart 1.1, assessing the "Relationship of Teaching Behaviors and Beliefs." List eight or ten processes you routinely employ in your teaching, such as "using examples from different cultural orientations to illustrate concepts, ideas, and skills." For each behavior listed, identify the underlying belief associated with it. Later on in the chapter you will have an opportunity to compare your values and beliefs or principles with those of other educators and to complete the third column.

Sources of Educational Principles

If educators are asked if there is a generally accepted set of principles of education to which their colleagues ascribe, they will probably agree that there is one. This ready response suggests that these principles should be easily identified by individuals and prominently discussed in the professional

Chart 1

Relationship of Teaching Behaviors and Beliefs		
Behavior	**Belief**	**Category of Principle**
Example: Routinely use multicultural examples to illustrate concepts for skills to be mastered by students.	Relevant teaching makes learning easier for students.	Teaching and Learning
Example: Expect all students to participate in multicultural learning experiences.	Multicultural education has benefits for all students, including European-Americans.	Teaching and Learning
1.		
2.		
3.		
4.		
5.		
6.		
7.		
8.		
9.		
10.		

literature. Operating on these assumptions, I gathered information from two sources to identify principles of general education in the United States: I conducted an informal survey, and I reviewed selected samples of educational literature. I did not ask any individuals to suggest principles of multicultural education but relied on the professional literature to generate these. I had two reasons for not asking for the latter principles. First, since multicultural education is still struggling for general acceptance, most educators would probably not be able to identify any of its principles. Second, many of the educators who could suggest some multicultural principles are specialists and proponents. Their thoughts and beliefs could be easily retrieved from professional writings.

The informal survey and literature review did not produce identical statements of educational principles. However, certain values and beliefs about the purpose, content, character, and process of education appeared repeatedly in both. The principles identified later in this chapter were extrapolated from the different explanations these sources generated about major U.S. values and why they are important for education and society. Although the principles were eventually compiled into a single list, the sources are discussed separately.

Suggestions from Individuals

I began the process of trying to identify a set of commonly accepted principles of general education by listing my own. I then proceeded to validate or refute them. To do this, I asked four different groups of educators to identify "two or three of what they considered to be the most fundamental principles or purposes of education in the United States." The four groups were college students enrolled in preservice teacher certification and graduate studies programs; suburban public school district superintendents; college professors engaged in teacher preparation; and personal friends involved in different levels of education. The last group included elementary and secondary teachers, district level administrators, counselors, and college professors. I was curious to see what different groups of educators would suggest and whether there would be any variance among them by role function and level of professional experience.

The individuals who participated in the informal survey varied in their professional experiences. Many had experienced long careers as teachers, administrators, and professors; as a group they were racially, ethnically, and regionally diverse, representing both genders. The group was not a representative random sample of the order that is required for empirical studies. Rather, this collection of individuals emerged from an impressionistic and intuitive impulse on my part as I sought to determine whether my beliefs about the major tenets of education in the United States were shared by others engaged in different aspects of education. The results indicated that there is, indeed, a high degree of consensus on the intended character and outcomes of U.S. education. As we will see later, this consensus was further substantiated by emphases found in the professional literature.

The survey produced a list of approximately 35 suggestions. Many of these overlapped or were repetitive. Most of the suggestions were phrases that signalled a value or belief rather than complete statements of actual principles. Certain ones were offered by many different individuals, including:

- Educational excellence for everyone.
- All students can learn.
- Teaching the whole child.
- Universal literacy.
- Teaching a universal set of values and the national culture.
- Capitalize on students' strengths.
- Equity and equality in education.
- Education for democratic citizenship.
- Every child is unique and has value.
- Develop the maximum potential of all students.
- Critical thinking skills.
- Preparation for future success.

In order to make the list more manageable, I reviewed it for clusters of similarity. Analysis of the beliefs about the nature and purpose of the educational process revealed four types of value orientations: *socialization, citizenship, human development,* and *effective teaching and learning.* These categories were used in reviewing the professional literature and in providing the framework for organizing the final list of principles.

Professional Literature

There are few writings in the body of educational scholarship that deal explicitly with principles of general education. A computer search of library sources produced none with this specific designation. Instead, principles of education tended to be embedded in discussions of other issues, such as the rights of students and teachers, school reform, learning theory, and democratic ideals. Writings on educational philosophy, psychology, and sociology deal far more frequently and explicitly with these beliefs than does the professional literature in curriculum planning and classroom teaching. The references included here are not the only available resources on educational principles. Rather, they are intended to represent various scholarly perspectives as well as explanations of values that undergird educational goals and practices in the United States. This sample of educational writings is also included to show how principles are embedded in, and often have to be extrapolated from, discussions about social values and educational goals, programs, and practices.

Categories of General Education Principles

Three categories of general education principles are introduced here and discussed in greater detail in Chapters 3 through 5: *human growth and development, citizenship and socialization,* and *teaching and learning.* There is a very close interaction between beliefs and ideas related to socialization—preparing students to be members of different groups—and citizenship—students' roles, rights, and responsibilities. These concepts are often discussed together under topics such as socialization for citizenship, democratic values, citizenship skills, and schools and society. Therefore, the principles of education for citizenship discussed here incorporate ideas about socialization.

The categories of educational principles approximate those used by other educators to identify and classify the major goals, visions, and values of U.S. education. Taba (1962), for example, summarized views about the functions of education under the three descriptors of *education as preservation and transmission of cultural heritage, education as an instrument for transforming culture,* and *education as a means for individual development.*

Human Growth and Development

Two themes that appear frequently in discussions of educational theory, philosophy, and practice are *individual development* and *personal empowerment* of students. They include ideas about how patterns of human growth and development should affect educational planning and practice, as well as how instructional programs should influence human development. Together they generate many important principles of education. Shor (1992) defined empowering education as a style of teaching that perceives the individual growth of students as an active, cooperative, and social process, since the self and society create each other. Its goals are to demonstrate how an individual's personal growth relates to public life and to develop strong, academic knowledge, habits of inquiry, and critical curiosity about how power, equality, and change operate in society. Obviously, the empowerment of students involves more than the mere transmission of cultural knowledge and the socialization of students into the existing social order. It engages students in change processes that combine knowledge, values, and actions to improve their own, as well as society's, well-being. Shor conceived education for empowerment as participatory, affective, problem-posing, situated, multicultural, dialogic, democratic, researching, interdisciplinary, and activist. Although this kind of education is difficult to achieve, it is absolutely essential for the healthy future of individuals and society. Shor (1992, 263) concluded his book with an eloquent statement that captures the flavor of the importance of education for personal empowerment and liberation:

> *Empowering education is thus a road from where we are to where we need to be. It crosses terrains of doubt and time. One end of the road leads away from inequality and miseducation while the other lands us in a frontier of critical learning and democratic discourse. This is no easy road to travel. Any place truly different from the status quo is not close by or down a simple trail. But the need to go there is evident, given what we know about unequal conditions and the decay in social life, given the need to replace teacher-talk and student alienation with dialogue and critical inquiry.*
>
> *Fortunately, some valuable resources already exist to democratize school and society. That transformation is a*

*journey of hope, humor, setbacks, breakthroughs, and
creative life, on a long and winding road paved with
dreams whose time is overdue.*

Many other educators agree. Hitt (1973) perceived education as a human
enterprise with a primary obligation to nurture the humanity of all students.
This belief is often transmitted through phrases such as "teaching the whole
child" and "helping students to become caring and sharing human beings."
According to Foshay (1970), attending to a student's "wholeness" requires
developing six dimensions of the human condition simultaneously. He identified these as the emotional, intellectual, social, aesthetic, spiritual, and biological. Other educators express the same idea as teaching to four domains of
learning—cognitive, affective, psychosocial, and performance. To accomplish
these goals, school programs and practices need to provide a variety of
options so that all students can participate fully and in multiple ways.

Hitt (1973) elaborated on these general ideas by identifying some
fundamentals of education that improve humanness. He described humans as
dualistic organisms, or what might loosely be called a combination of internal
and external, rational and intuitive, mental and emotional, scientific and
humanistic, and objective and existential dimensions. For example, humans:
are objects of observation and they study others; receive and create knowledge; live by reason and faith; are individually unique but very similar; and
exist as complete individuals yet are in a constant state of development.
Education programs and practices should cultivate both ends of the "continua
of being." Hitt believed that 10 key indicators of humanness could form the
core of all education: identity, authenticity, communication, reason, problem
solving, concern for others, independence, open-mindedness, responsibility,
and zest for life.

Thelen (1970) provided another image of the "humane" person that
schools should work to develop and that society needs in order to flourish. It
complements the ones constructed by both Foshay (1970) and Hitt (1973).
Thelen defined humane persons as those who (1) are actively involved in their
culture and contribute to its further refinement; (2) have a clear understanding
of the relationship between individual and universal human needs; (3) have a
strong sense of history and an appreciation of humanity's continuing struggle

Table 1.1

Educational Principles Related to Human Growth and Development

- Education must be comprehensive and multidimensional in order to be congruent with the interrelated and holistic nature of human growth and development.
- Educational programs and practices must be flexible in order to accommodate the different rates of growth among the various aspects of human development.
- Education should create learning environments and experiences that enhance the learning preferences and styles of students.
- Education should lead to greater individual social and intellectual freedom for all students.
- Education should improve the self-acceptance of students.
- Education should build upon the personal strengths and abilities of students.
- Education practices should be organized to match the sequence of human growth and development.
- Educational programs and practices should allow for different kinds of internal and external motivations for learning.
- Education should use diverse means to achieve the universal ends of humankind.
- Educational practices should provide variety in learning experiences to accommodate the variability in human growth and development.
- Educational practices should promote the human dignity of all students.
- Education should consider the role of cultural influences in human growth and development.

for improvement; and (4) are citizens of a society interactively involved with their social and natural environments. Students become more humane when schools and teachers act as facilitators in their search for self-discovery, rather than telling students what to think, believe, know, and do.

From these ideas emerges another key principle of education as a human enterprise: students should be the primary architects of their own learning, with teachers providing supportive guidance and assistance. When schools accept these challenges and redefine their roles accordingly, they too will become more truly humane institutions, with the human fulfillment of individual students being the prevailing theme. This, in turn, will lead to a more humanistic and democratic society (Hitt 1973).

Several familiar principles of U.S. education are derived from these

Albuquerque Academy Library

values concerning the nature of the process of growth and development common to most individuals and its influence on educational decision making. Some of these principles are listed in Table 1.1.

Citizenship and Socialization

Phenix's writings illustrate how educational scholars integrate beliefs about education for citizenship and socialization. In 1961 he published a moral philosophy for school curriculum, which gave priority to socialization and citizenship. Phenix suggested that the major principles of U.S. education could be discerned from the nation's democratic philosophy. In fact, education is the foundation of democracy, and democracy is the ultimate outcome of education. Both are grounded in principles of freedom, equality, and justice. These are essentially moral imperatives, since democracy rather than being a political structure is more a philosophical ideal and social system in which all individuals are considered to be equal in significant ways. However, this does not mean that all people have the same abilities, interests, needs, or circumstances. They are equal in being human, mortal, possessed of body, mind, and spirit, and they are engaged in a continuing search for truth, right, and goodness. The challenge of schools in a democratic society is to seek out greater freedom and justice for the common good and to develop strong feelings of national loyalty. Teaching and learning should be characterized by analysis, reflection, dialogue, and social action. Even though the content of this common good is not yet fully known or fully agreed upon,

> *education for democracy . . . should encourage the habit of sustained inquiry and the art of sincere persuasion, and . . . confirm and celebrate faith in the priority . . . of truth and goodness, in which the moral enterprise is grounded* (Phenix 1961).

Therefore, all parts of the educational process have a moral obligation to model and teach principles of democracy.

Gardner (1984) made basically the same point as Phenix about the interaction between text and context of educational values and beliefs. He explained that in a pluralistic society like that of the United States we should expect to have a great deal of diversity of values, opinions, goals, and behaviors among individuals and groups with regard to personal priorities and the common good. However, this does not mean that there is no consensus about the aims of education for a democratic society. United States citizens from different ethnic identities, social classes, and cultural backgrounds support the ideal values of peace, justice, freedom, human dignity, equality, and the pursuit of excellence. Furthermore, Gardner (1984, 82–83) contended:

> *We believe that men and women should be enabled to achieve the best that is in them, and we are the declared enemies of all conditions . . . that stunt the individual and prevent such fulfillment.*

Exactly what is "the best" for different individuals—and opinions about how to eliminate conditions that interfere with its realization—vary widely. Educational programs and practices should be conceived broadly enough to accommodate this diversity instead of imposing a few narrow visions of excellence upon everyone.

Some educators find it challenging to apply Phenix's mandates in ethnically diverse and culturally pluralistic school settings. Their anxiety is relieved somewhat by remembering that "there is nothing . . . intrinsically incompatible between democratic principles and multi-ethnic living" (Sigel 1991, 3). Nor should we assume that students will learn how to live democratically in a multiethnic, multicultural, and multiracial society and world without being taught how to do so. All students must learn these skills, not just recent immigrants, groups of color, children of poverty, or limited English speakers. They must learn to value the lives and cultures of different groups "without blindly assuming that their own culture is superior, and therefore immune to change or improvement" (Sigel 1991, 6).

Shapiro and Purpel (1993) offered a different viewpoint of the major values that direct our society and schools. They suggested that capitalism is the driving force that energizes all dimensions of society. Consequently, approaches to schooling in the United States cannot be understood fully without a careful analysis of capitalistic values.

Cagan (1978) analyzed how U.S. individualism is shaped by a capitalistic philosophy that generates social relations that are competitive, egotistical, and self-serving. She warned that "such relations are inimical to the development of true individuality and human liberation and must be deliberately offset by a pedagogy that adheres to collective goals" (Cagan 1978, 228).

Bianchi (1975, 45) described capitalism as the "total environment in which we are reared and conditioned," not just an economic system. Its values of personal initiative, competition, individualism, and consumerism are not so much concerned with promoting the emotional, intellectual, ethical, and cultural growth of individuals as they are with maximizing individual profits and gains. Bianchi perceived these priorities as a variation of the social Darwinist idea of "survival of the fittest," which is contradictory to other U.S. values that stress the creation of community among individuals. He explained that "possession of material goods is still the clearest sign of 'fitness.' To possess more is to be more worthy as a person" (Bianchi 1975, 46–47). While lip service is given to the ethics and morality of the techniques used to

Table 1.2

Principles of Education for Citizenship and Socialization
◆ Public and free education is a basic human right of all children.
◆ Education should teach students to become social change agents as individuals and members of groups with common interests and causes.
◆ Education for social consciousness, personal well-being, and community building is essential for democratic citizenship.
◆ Education for responsible citizenship involves cultivating knowledge, values, behaviors, ethics, and morality consistent with democratic ideals.
◆ Education should model the values of freedom, equality, dignity, enfranchisement, and justice.
◆ Education should teach students to understand the interdependent and interactive relationships between individuals, groups, and environments.
◆ Education should promote intolerance of all forms of discrimination, oppression, and exploitation.
◆ Education should teach students how to create national unity and a common culture out of individual and group diversity.
◆ Education should teach students to respect, value, and celebrate individual ethnic, cultural, social, racial, and linguistic diversity.

become successful, respecting and protecting the humaneness of self and others in the drive toward capitalistic success are minimized or ignored entirely. "In this milieu, to be human is to be violent toward nature, self and others. For only the respectably aggressive will possess goods, status and selfhood" (Bianchi 1975, 47).

Advertising is a graphic example of how capitalistic values are transmitted. There is a persistent socialization subtext in all advertising that is as important as the one designed to sell the product or service. According to Shapiro and Purpel (1993), this subtext teaches consumers that the more they buy, the happier and more fulfilled they will be, and the better they will be able to deal with such fundamental human concerns as sociability, sexuality, security, gender role identity, and physical well-being. Conversely, those who are less able to buy can expect to be less successful, both as persons and citizens.

In schools, students are taught similar values in many subtle and explicit ways. They are nested in the emphasis we place on competition for grades, awards and recognitions, test scores, and an academic caste system perpetuated through tracking. The underlying message is that everyone can succeed with proper skills and individual initiative. This idea is often expressed in contemporary educational theory as "all students *can* learn." However, not all students *do* learn because some lack the necessary motivation and skills. These beliefs are sometimes referred to as the "principle of meritocracy."

Several specific principles of education related to socialization and citizenship emerge from these explanations and similar ones found in professional literature. They are summarized in Table 1.2.

Teaching and Learning

While principles of education about socialization, citizenship, and humanism relate to the desired "products" or outcomes of schooling, those about teaching and learning focus on making "process features" most effective. They include beliefs about the best ways to facilitate learning of the knowledge and skills essential for socialization, citizenship, and human development.

Most educators in the United States view teaching and learning as being interactive and reciprocal. That is, the characteristics of learners and how they engage in the learning process are major factors in determining how teaching is organized and executed. Other common thoughts about learning are: (1) the level and quality of current learning are affected by prior experiences; (2) learning is an active process in which students are engaged in creating, selecting, and organizing information and experiences into new structures of meaning; (3) learning is a "whole" process involving the "total" person; (4) learning is essentially a social process that requires learners to interact with others; and (5) learning is enhanced by motivation, interest, and practice (Hilgard and Bower 1975; Taba 1962).

Although learning is a social process, individual differences affect learning significantly. Each individual brings a unique set of experiences to learning situations, influencing how each responds to current teaching encounters. Classroom programs and practices should build upon these personal differences and preceding experiences. Because this continuity is an essential

Table 1.3

Principles of Teaching and Learning
◆ Learning is more effective when the ways and environments in which children learn match their personal preferences.
◆ Providing academic access, equity, and excellence for all students is a moral obligation of education.
◆ Learning is more effective when students are involved in cooperative, collaborative, and mutually supportive experiences.
◆ Education should empower students through knowledge acquisition, moral conviction, social consciousness, and political activism.
◆ Child-centered program planning and instructional practices improve the quality of educational opportunities and outcomes for all students.
◆ Education should promote high standards and expectations of achievement for all students.
◆ Educational content and processes should reflect the perspectives and contributions of all citizens of the United States.
◆ Diversity and flexibility in curriculum and instruction are needed to accommodate the different readiness levels, developmental rates, learning styles, and intellectual abilities of students.
◆ Education should expand the personal, social, intellectual, and experiential horizons of all children.
◆ Relevant teaching methods and materials increase student mastery of content and skills taught.
◆ Positive self-concept and self-esteem are necessary conditions and companions of academic achievement.

condition of learning, curriculum and instruction should provide cumulative learning opportunities for students.

These concepts about learning have direct implications for planning and implementing instructional programs. Taba (1962) identified several significant ones. First, more importance is assigned to cognitive processes, understanding contexts and relationships, problem-solving techniques, creativity, and inquiry learning than to knowledge of isolated facts. Second, the act of learning is viewed as a *transaction* between the learner and the content to be learned. This means students question, explore, critique, and analyze all forms of knowledge they encounter in the learning process. Specific content has relative value. It is important only to the extent that it is part of a meaningful context, serves a given purpose, helps to shape particular mental processes, and leads to the formation of new ideas. Third, learning with understanding is best achieved by using a variety of instructional materials and techniques that

Table 1.3 (continued)

- Maximizing the human development of students requires teaching the whole child.
- Learning is easier and lasts longer when the tasks are developmentally appropriate for the students.
- The quality of student learning efforts and outcomes should be judged on individual merits.
- Mastery of basic literacy skills is imperative for all students.
- Critical thinking and problem-solving skills are essential to the personal growth of individuals and the continual development of society.
- Transmitting the cumulative knowledge of humankind and the national culture to students is a fundamental purpose of education.
- Learning generated from intrinsic motivation is retained longer than that stimulated by external motivation.
- Education for social change is both desirable and imperative.
- Learning with understanding is more thorough, permanent, and transferable than learning that is by rote or by formula.
- Learning is culturally relative and is affected by significant influences from both the macroculture and microcultures to which students belong.
- The continuous search for scholarly truth is a valid goal and characteristic of the educational process.
- Knowledge should be understood as a form of cultural capital and a significant source of personal and social power.

have personal meaning for different students. Fourth, frequent opportunities are provided for students to be active participants in the decision-making processes about what, why, and how they will learn.

Walker and Soltis (1992) extrapolated other directions for designing curriculum and classroom instruction from such common values of U.S. culture as individuality, freedom, progress, conformity, and change. They advised that educational goals and practices must offer a variety of teaching and learning techniques in order to prepare students for "new conditions and emerging social values . . . to cultivate knowledge, to sustain and improve society, and to foster the well-being of individuals" (Walker and Soltis 1992, 82). Each of these is important to some degree in the education of all students, but how they are achieved varies widely. Thus, diversity in curriculum and instruction is the best way to prepare all students for the wide variety of situations and experiences they will encounter in life and to be effective and responsible members of a democratic society. Embedded within these two general ideals are several more specific roles for schools and teachers: facilitating intelligent and critical thinking; relating schooling to living; contextualizing basic and cultural literacies for different groups and situations; perceiving education as an instrument of societal development; and recognizing that it is important for all students to learn a common core of historical, social, and scientific knowledge (Walker and Soltis 1992).

Taba (1962, 25) added another perspective for identifying principles of teaching and learning in the United States. She reminded us that:

> *education must, and usually does, work in the cultural setting of a given society, at a given time, in a given place, shaping individuals in some measure to participate in that society. . . . The decision-makers themselves are immersed in the culture and therefore subject to the culturally conditioned conceptions of how education is to serve that society. . . . Education must adjust its aims and programs to changing conditions . . . Without a continual reorientation to changing conditions, education becomes unreal and, in a sense, useless because it does not prepare youth for life's problems and responsibilities.*

From the ideas of Taba, Walker and Soltis, Hilgard and Bower, and others, including the individuals who participated in the informal survey, emerged principles of education that addressed what knowledge is of most value, the best ways of knowing, and the most effective ways of teaching. Some of these are presented in Table 1.3 on pages 24 and 25.

Reflections and Applications

Several attributes of general education principles evolve from the discussions in this chapter. First, they address elements of individual and social development. For the sake of analysis, these were examined separately, but in actual practice they are closely interrelated. It is almost impossible to talk about values, goals, and processes of education for individual development without placing these within some kind of social context.

Schools are doubly social in nature: they are created by society to educate its youth, and the materials that constitute the core of school programs are drawn from the society in which they exist (Taba 1962). These relationships become more apparent in Chapters 3 to 5 as principles of education for human growth and development, citizenship and socialization, and teaching and learning are discussed in more detail.

A second attribute of general education principles is their close similarity to the values of the national culture. Most educational principles are grounded in the democratic ideals of freedom, equality, justice, and human dignity and the capitalistic ideas of individual worth, competition, progress, and success. This is not surprising since education is always culturally relative.

Change is a consistent theme in descriptions of our society and in visions of U.S. education. Consequently, many educational principles are, third, prescriptive, in that they emphasize "where we need to be" as individuals and as a society. They have within them elements of cultural transmission, social transformation, and individual actualization.

A fourth attribute of principles of general education is evident in the emphasis given to concepts about teaching and learning. Thoughts about what is worth learning and how learning can best be achieved invariably focus on process over content, skills instead of facts, and how to learn and teach rather than what to learn and teach.

Several suggestions are offered below to help you to further clarify and extend your understanding of the relationship between principles of general education and principles of multicultural education. Others suggest ways to begin to apply these understandings in classroom practice.

1. Now that you have had a chance to consider what selected educators believe are the major principles of general education, compare them with your own. Return to the chart entitled "Relationship of Teaching Behaviors and Beliefs" (page 13) that you completed at the beginning of this chapter. Examine it carefully and compare your beliefs with those identified throughout this chapter, and then determine what types of principles are embedded in each. Did your beliefs and values about the goals and processes of education fall into the same categories (human growth and development, citizenship and socialization, and teaching and learning)? In the third column of the chart, place the appropriate category of principles opposite each of your suggested behaviors and beliefs.

2. Sometimes educational reform does not move forward as quickly and successfully as it might because educators do not necessarily share a common vision and often end up working at cross-purposes. Is this the situation in your school environment? If you are already teaching, ask 15 to 20 other teachers, counselors, and administrators to (1) identify what they consider to be the five most important kinds of content areas or skills students should learn; and (2) explain the reasons for their choices. If you are in college, the same questions can be asked of students and professors in different areas of specialization, such as education, engineering, liberal arts, and sciences. After you have collected the comments, compare them by respondents and their job functions (i.e., teachers with counselors and administrators), and by the categories and types of principles (i.e., human growth and development, citizenship and socialization, and teaching and learning). Then, determine the degree to which the different groups are consistent or in agreement.

3. Create a primer of "Ten Principles of Education To Guide Classroom Practice." Select principles from those described in this chapter. Give two or three examples of classroom actions generated by each of your principles. For instance, "Diversity and flexibility in curriculum and instruction are needed to accommodate different readiness levels, developmental rates, learning styles, and intellectual abilities of students" might be associated with these behavioral examples: (1) Students can choose to write, tell, or perform their skill mastery when I do achievement assessment; (2) I routinely use several different kinds of sensory stimulation (reading, listening, viewing, acting) to teach facts, concepts, ideas, and skills; and (3) My students have frequent opportunities to practice what they learn through individual assignments, peer teaching, cooperative groupwork, and large-group instruction. You can involve your students as active partners in creating the primers. Explain what each principle means. Then, ask your students to provide examples of your teaching that they feel represent each principle. Or, depending on their maturity level, ask them to extrapolate principles from your classroom practices. This is a good way to find out if your students perceive your instructional values and practices the same way you do. Once the primers are completed, distribute them to your students and their parents as a means of communicating your beliefs about the most important goals and values that guide your classroom practices.

4. Develop a bibliography of children's and young adults' literature that reflects the categories identified and elaborated on in this chapter. Your bibliography should:

• Have a total of 10–15 entries distributed across the themes of human growth and development, citizenship and socialization, and teaching and learning.

• Include an annotation for each entry, telling the theme illustrated by each literature sample.

• Be pluralistic; entries should represent different ethnic, racial, and cultural groups and experiences.

• Include multiple literary genres (novels, poetry, essays, drama, short stories, song lyrics) and literary categories (fiction, nonfiction, autobiographies).

Some of your selections will probably deal with more than one of the themes, but your complete list should still include 10–15 items. You may have to use a few professional books or articles, especially for the teaching and learning theme. However, these should be the exception, since the focus of the bibliography should be children's literature. If you teach middle school, high school, or college students, have them *analytically* read the selections in your bibliography to see if they can discern the cultural values and educational principles embedded in them.

References

Banks, C. A. M. 1993. Restructuring schools for equity: What we have learned in two decades. *Phi Delta Kappan* 75(1): 42–48.

Bianchi, E. C. 1989. The gospel way and the American way are contradictory. In *American values: Opposing viewpoints*, ed. D. L. Bender, 44–49. San Diego, Calif.: Greenhaven Press.

Brandwein, P. F. 1981. *Memorandum: On renewing schooling and education*. New York: Harcourt Brace Jovanovich.

Cagan, E. 1978. Individualism, collectivism, and radical educational reform. *Harvard Educational Review* 48(2): 227–66.

Foshay, A. W. 1970. Curriculum development and the humane qualities. In *To nurture humaneness: Commitment for the '70's,* ed. M. M. Scobey and G. Graham, 143–53. Washington, D.C.: Association for Supervision and Curriculum Development.

Gardner, J. W. 1984. *Excellence*. New York: Norton.

Hilgard, E. R., and G. H. Bower. 1975. *Theories of learning*. Englewood Cliffs, N.J.: Prentice-Hall.

Hitt, W. D. 1973. *Education as a human enterprise*. Worthington, Ohio: Charles A. Jones Publishing Company.

Mason, R. E. 1960. *Educational ideals in American society*. Boston: Allyn and Bacon.

Phenix, P. H. 1961. *Education and the common good: A moral philosophy of the curriculum*. New York: Harper and Brothers.

Shapiro, H. S., and D. E. Purpel, eds. 1993. *Critical social issues in American education: Toward the 21st century*. New York: Longman.

Shor, I. 1992. *Empowering education: Critical teaching for social change*. Chicago: The University of Chicago Press.

Sigel, R. S. 1991. Democracy in the multi-ethnic society. In *Education for democratic citizenship: A challenge for multi-ethnic societies*, eds. R. S. Sigel and M. Hoskin, 3–8. Hillsdale, N.J.: Lawrence Erlbaum Associates.

Taba, H. 1962. *Curriculum development: Theory and practice*. New York: Harcourt, Brace and World.

Thelen, H. A. 1970. Comments on "What it means to be humane." In *To nurture humaneness: Commitment for the '70's,* ed. M. M. Scobey and G. Graham, 27–32. Washington, D.C.: Association for Supervision and Curriculum Development.

Walker, D. F., and J. F. Soltis. 1986. *Curriculum and aims*. New York: Teachers College Press, Columbia University.

Chapter 2

Perspectives and Principles of Multicultural Education

In periods of crisis the question of the central function of schools in society becomes a subject of heated controversy, with the nature of the relationships of education to society at the very core of that controversy.

(Taba 1962, 17)

We need leaders and educators of good will, from all political and ideological persuasions, to participate in genuine discussions, dialogues, and debates that will help us formulate visionary and workable solutions and enable us to deal creatively with the challenges posed by the increasing diversity in the United States and the world. We must learn to transform the problems related to racial and ethnic diversity into opportunities and strengths.

(Banks 1994, 3)

The mere mention of multicultural education evokes a variety of reactions and images among educators. The reaction varies both within and among groups of proponents and critics and ranges along a continuum of intensity from gentility to militancy, from conservative to radical. Some educators only perceive problems with multicultural education and predict collisions between it and the efforts and goals of general education; others see complementary, enriching, and interactive relationships between multicultural education and general education. The position one takes in this debate reflects certain kinds of philosophical beliefs about the place of cultural diversity in education, and that position has a profound effect on the identification and interpretation of the perceived values, benefits, nature, and purposes—that is, the principles—of multicultural education.

What about you? How do you react when you hear the term *multicultural education?* Do you feel doubt, joy, frustration, confusion, fear, excitement, ambiguity, incompetence, or opportunity? Perhaps the term evokes memories of specific experiences, such as a movie you saw, a lesson you taught, a curriculum reform project in your school district, a professional conference you attended, or a new student who just arrived in your classroom. What kinds of images cross your mental screens? Might these include cultural festivals, special holiday celebrations, hostilities among diverse groups, "rainbow coalitions" with diverse groups engaged harmoniously in common causes, or everyday people doing everyday things? Do you think of multicultural education as planting seeds of construction or of destruction, as limiting or increasing the potential of individuals and society? Do you wonder if your thoughts, feelings, and images are "correct," and shared by other teachers? Or, do you wonder if you stand alone?

If you have not thought about these kinds of questions before, take time to do so now. If you have already begun to think about them, keep them in the forefront of your mind as you read this chapter. The information presented may affirm some of your thoughts and positions, clarify others, and provide some insights that you have not considered previously. At the least, it will undoubtedly demonstrate that you are not alone in whatever positions you take on multicultural education.

This chapter explores some of the major arguments for and against multicultural education and its connection to general education. The focus is more on the major principles than on the practices of multicultural education. The intent is to explain why critics contend that these principles contradict those of general education and why proponents argue that multicultural education and general education are highly compatible and complementary.

Parameters of the Controversy

Multicultural education is a very controversial idea, and the debate over it is gaining widespread national attention. It is controversial because there are so many different notions about what it is, how it should be implemented, and where it fits into the overall scheme of education in the United States. It also challenges how some of the nation's most fundamental value assumptions have been interpreted and translated into action. Interest in it is becoming more and more widespread, not because it is commonly accepted, but because ethnic and cultural diversity is growing in magnitude and influence in all segments of society. People in government, business, economic institutions, religion, media, and the entertainment industry are asking questions about how to deal effectively with ethnically and culturally diverse issues and audiences in their respective areas of interest. Consider, for example, how frequently ethnic events dominate newspaper headlines and prime-time television newscasts. Or how often businesses engage in "segmented marketing" to make their goods and services more appealing to different racial, ethnic, and gender groups.

Changes occurring in the ethnic demographics of the United States are so widespread and important that William Henry (1990) dubbed them "the browning of America." He suggested that increased tensions between ethnic groups over economic and political resources are unavoidable. However, the greater challenge of this diversity is "what it means to the national psyche, to individuals' sense of themselves and their nation—their idea of what it is to be American" (Henry 1990, 30). Rather than accept without question the until-now standard renditions of the history of the United States and its culture, these diverse citizens will more freely debate the sources of the nation's strength and success, the compositon of its unalterable beliefs, and the identity of those with the right to define popular culture.

This is not the first time in the history of the United States that groups and individuals who were denied access to mainstream institutions and opportunities have questioned prevailing norms and practices. In fact, this was the impetus behind the birth of our nation and its phenomenal rise to international prominence. From Europeans who settled in the New World to escape the quality of life in their native lands, to African slaves who refused to accept bondage as their destiny, to the Civil Rights Movement of the last 40 years, diverse groups have demanded that our society and institutions be inclusive and accessible to all the peoples who contributed in their making.

A major part of the controversy surrounding multicultural education stems from questions about how to reconcile its emphasis on diversity with the values of unity symbolized by the national motto, *e pluribus unum*. According to Banks (1993), a leading proponent, the debate is framed by three commonly held misconceptions—that multicultural education is: (1) an entitlement program and curriculum movement only for and about groups of color, the powerless, women, and other "victims"; (2) contradictory to Western cultural and democratic ideals; and (3) a divisive force that will destroy the national unity. Other dimensions of the controversy revolve around questions such as: Will studying cultural differences aggravate existing hostilities between ethnic and racial groups or even create new ones? Aren't schools obligated to teach a national common culture to all students? If we concentrate on cultural pluralism in schools, will there be enough time left to teach such fundamentals as literacy, critical thinking, problem solving, and the various subject matter skills? How can teachers be expected to teach the culture of so many groups when, in some instances, there are 15 or more different ethnic groups and languages represented in a single classroom and even more in a school? These questions are at the heart of what might be called an *ideological* or *valuative* debate, since they ask us to determine the "right" and "best" ways to educate students from a wide variety of ethnic and cultural backgrounds.

Davidman and Davidman (1994) identified six contributing factors helpful in understanding the controversy surrounding multicultural education:

1. As a reform movement, multicultural education punctures theories and beliefs of individuals comfortable with and interested in maintaining the existing social order.
2. Multicultural educators offer a new vision of what it means to be an American, which threatens old notions of national strength and unity.
3. Multicultural education challenges those individuals who view the United States as a monocultural society built around human values. It suggests that a universalistic, "one world, one people" viewpoint is inflexible and promotes the cultural ethnocentricism of European-Americans.
4. Multicultural education's emphasis on equity causes some people to perceive it as a threat, reducing the resources available to other important programs.
5. Many people find the antiracist theme in multicultural education difficult and intimidating to embrace. They view teaching about racism as a highly explosive and volatile undertaking that they prefer to avoid.
6. The multifaceted nature of multicultural education generates diverse conceptions that sometimes cause division among its proponents. This apparent lack of consensus is often inter-

preted by critics or skeptics as a weakness that causes the
integrity and validity of multicultural education to be suspect.

Another major point of controversy can be added to the list provided by
Davidman and Davidman: Multicultural education challenges how the basic
assumptions and beliefs we hold about education in the United States are
interpreted and practiced. Many educators misunderstand this challenge and
conclude that multicultural education is disavowing the beliefs themselves
instead of how they are understood and practiced. A case in point is the idea
that all students can learn and have the right to a high-quality education.
Multiculturalists support this belief as strongly as other educators do. Differences begin to appear in discussions about what to do in practice to achieve
it. Many educators feel that all students should be exposed to the same
educational practices in the same ways to ensure high-quality learning opportunities. Multicultural educators believe that treating all students the same is a
philosophical mandate, not a practical one. When it comes to classroom practices, variety and diversity of instructional methods that reflect cultural and
ethnic sensitivity must be used in teaching students from different racial,
social, linguistic, and ancestral backgrounds. Thus, advocates of multicultural
education argue that cultural diversity must be a fundamental part of all components of the educational process, including curriculum, instruction, administration, counseling, evaluation, and school climate, and it must be accessible
to all students.

By comparison, some critics contend that there is no place for cultural
diversity in the curriculum of public schools. They feel that the purpose of
public education is to teach students about the common national culture, with
an emphasis on similarities and unity. Other critics concede that students
should learn about cultural diversity, but they restrict the learning to lessons
and units added to existing curriculum. They would be receptive to selective
efforts to teaching about cultural diversity, such as having a cultural fair of folk
customs and cuisines at the end of a social studies unit on immigration. They
would advocate adding books by Japanese-Americans, Latinos, Native Americans, and African-Americans to a language arts unit on novels. These critics
would also limit learning about cultural diversity to students in schools with
large percentages of students of color, such as large urban centers. They see

no place for multicultural education and cultural pluralism in suburban and rural schools with predominantly European-American student populations.

Many classroom teachers do not like to become embroiled in arguments about educational ideals, preferring instead to focus on instructional strategies. Yet educational values, ideals, and behaviors are not separate entities; their relationship is reciprocal. The beliefs and values that drive the controversy surrounding multicultural education have a direct influence on decisions educators make about curriculum design, instructional strategies, and teaching materials. Therefore, it is important for all educators to be consciously aware of what some of these beliefs and values are. The major points of contention between critical and advocacy perspectives on multicultural education are summarized below. This knowledge will help you better understand your own priorities, as well as why your school district and colleagues may prefer certain strategies over others, including, perhaps, deciding to do nothing about multicultural education.

Critical Perspectives

Skeptics and critics of multicultural education fall into four major categories—the conservative right, the radical left, moderates, and the undecided. Despite differences in emphasis and points of analysis, most critics of multicultural education tend to center their arguments on what they consider the negative social consequences associated with teaching about ethnic and cultural pluralism and the questionable quality of multicultural scholarship.

Prominent among the conservative critics of multicultural education are Chester Finn, Dinesh D'Souza, Diane Ravitch, Arthur Schlesinger, and William Bennett. These opponents feel that multicultural education contradicts the basic purposes of U.S. schooling, which are: to teach students skills to participate in the shared national culture; to promote allegiance to the values of the nation; to become competent in English; and to ensure national unity. They see the demand that education include the contributions of all cultures and ethnic groups as an attempt by racial minorities to destroy the Western European cultural heritage on which the United States was founded. A brief summary of Schlesinger, Ravitch, and D'Souza's specific ideas on these general issues is included here as representative of the type of arguments conservative critics offer against teaching cultural diversity and multicultural education.

The type of language Schlesinger (1992) used in *The Disuniting of America* to express his views on multicultural education is as revealing as the substance of its messages. Schlesinger repeatedly used phrases like "cult of ethnicity," "new ethnic gospel," and "multiethnic dogma" to refer to the increasing levels of ethnic group identity, association, activism, and demand for multicultural education. He conceded that "the eruption of ethnicity" has had some positive consequences, such as helping Americans realize that they are citizens of a shrinking world and that there is a need to learn much more about other races, cultures, and countries. But he pointed out that when carried to extremes, emphases on differences can have serious negative effects. Schlesinger identified some of these as rejecting the vision of unifying individuals from all national origins into a single nation and culture, decreasing interest in integration and assimilation, and increasing levels of segregation and separatism among ethnic and racial groups. He stated that these demands have already transformed the United States "into a more segregated society . . . imposed ethnocentric, Afrocentric, and bilingual curricula in public schools . . . filled the air with recrimination and rancor and have remarkably advanced the fragmentation of American life" (Schlesinger 1992, 130). As a result, racial prejudices are being nourished, and antagonisms between groups are flourishing. He also said that cultural diversity is the aspiration of only a few ethnic individuals because most "American-born members of minority groups, white or nonwhite . . . still see themselves primarily as Americans" (Schlesinger 1992, 19), even though they may selectively cherish their particular cultural heritage.

Ravitch (1990) agreed with Schlesinger's contentions that advocating cultural diversity is a threat to national unity and cohesion. She called the demands by groups of color for the inclusion of their histories, cultures, and contributions in school curricula "ethnic particularism." She described it as an:

> *'unabashedly filiopietistic' notion which teaches children*
> *that their identity is determined by their 'cultural genes.'*
> *That something in their blood or race memory or their*
> *cultural DNA determines who they are and what they may*
> *achieve. That they must immerse themselves in their*
> *'native' culture in order to understand subject matter that*

is taught in school. That the culture they live in is not their
native culture. That American culture is Eurocentric

and therefore hostile to anyone whose ancestors are not European (Ravitch 1990, 46–47). In her estimation these demands deny the fact that ethnics of color are a part of mainstream U.S. society, and they may actually damage the self-esteem of racial minority children and intensify their sense of marginalization in the national culture.

D'Souza (1991) presented his criticisms of multicultural education in *Illiberal Education*. They evolved out of his assessment of college-level ethnic minority and women studies. D'Souza described these programs as "bullying pedagogy" and "tyranny of the minority," creating a "monolithic ideological focus that places minority sentiments on a pedestal while putting majority ones on trial" (1991, 214–15). He questioned the intellectual rigor of these programs and suggested that they are more "ethnic and female cheerleading" than scholarly investigations. He supported the contention of other critics that the study of cultural differences is divisive and is intended to destroy the European-based heritages of the United States.

At the other end of the spectrum of opposition to multicultural education are leftist critics. Referred to in the professional literature as "the radical critique," these opponents have been much more vocal in England, Canada, and Australia than in the United States. Among the leading spokespersons are Brian Bullivant (1984; 1986) from Australia, Mike Cole (1992) and Chris Mullard (1984) from England, and Cameron McCarthy (1988) from the United States. They believe multicultural education does not deal aggressively enough with race, class, and gender oppression, political and economic inequities, and the institutional structures of society. Instead, it places too much emphasis on cultural studies, race relations, insignificant cultural artifacts (such as folk heroes, festivals, foods, holidays, and traditional practices), isolated historical events, and improving self-concepts. Radical critics decry as simplistic and naive the assumption that teaching children of color about their cultural heritage will improve their academic achievement and ultimately lead to better employment. To them these emphases are "trivial pursuits" that ignore the more important issues of power, poverty, and racism in education and their pervasive negative influences for ethnic minorities. McCarthy (1988, 269) added that "by focusing on sensitivity training and on individual differences, multicultural proponents typically skirt the very problem which multicultural education seeks to address: WHITE RACISM." Multicultural education creates a convenient smokescreen or illusion of change that allows the dominant society to continue to deny minority groups the political power and economic resources needed to improve the quality of their lives. It placates ethnic minorities and lulls them into the false belief that cross-cultural understanding will lead to more social equity (Bullivant 1984; 1986; Cole 1992; McCarthy 1988). Therefore, a more appropriate programmatic goal and focus for schools is *antiracist education.* All curriculum content, learning experiences, and instructional strategies should emphasize liberation for oppressed groups, social action for social justice, redistribution of political and economic power, and developing skills for combating the insidious ways in which racism is practiced, maintained, and reproduced (Cole 1992; Leicester 1992; Troyna 1987).

John Ogbu's (1992) criticisms of multicultural education represent a moderate position in comparison with those of the conservative right and the radical left. An anthropologist who studies the relationship between education, ethnicity, and social class, Ogbu is known for his distinctions between voluntary and involuntary minorities. His critiques attend more to pedagogical or instructional issues than those of many other critics. In two recent articles, Ogbu (1991; 1992) expressed strong reservations about the academic potential of multicultural education. He doubted whether it would bring about any appreciable changes in the academic performance of those involuntary racial minority groups, such as African-Americans, Latinos, and Native Americans, who traditionally have performed poorly in schools. His reasons for taking this position included that multicultural education: (1) tends to ignore the responsibility of ethnic minority students for their own learning; (2) is rarely based on thorough studies of minority groups within their own cultural communities; (3) does not distinguish clearly between minority groups who achieve academic success and those who do not; and (4) is not sufficiently informed about how the home cultures and languages of racial minorities affect their learning efforts and outcomes.

A fourth group of educators who are not unequivocal supporters of multicultural education might be called the "undecided." They are more skeptical than critical. These individuals are not so much philosophically opposed to multicultural education as they are genuinely puzzled about how to implement it in the classroom. They may recognize that the education system is failing to meet the needs of some ethnically and culturally different students and that an undercurrent of racial hostility prevails among students, but they do not know what to do about these problems. This was the situation at a middle school in Bellevue, Washington, which appealed to me for help. The principal explained that the ethnic diversity in the student population had changed radically in the last two years. Most members of the teaching staff, which was 99 percent European-American, were encountering for the first time in many years of professional experience African-American, Latino, Korean-American, Filipino-American, Cambodian-American, Vietnamese-American, and Laotian-American students. The students exhibited attitudes and behaviors that the teachers did not understand and that they often perceived as negative and hostile. Some teachers actually feared the students.

The teachers were genuine in their appeal for help, yet they were reluctant to accept suggestions that the solutions to their problems might be found in applying multicultural education strategies in their teaching and interactions with students. Explanations of strategies, such as using culturally different examples and materials to teach concepts and skills and changing teaching techniques to match different ethnic learning styles were met with skepticism. Teachers raised predictable questions about whether these strategies might: lower academic standards; seem unfair and discriminatory; cause European-American students to resent being left out; and cause students of color to feel teachers are intruding in their lives. These are common responses of European-American teachers to multicultural education (Howard 1993). Embedded in these reactions are denial, fear, guilt, and even hostility.

Educators with these kinds of reactions and concerns are so confused, uncertain, overwhelmed, or overburdened that they hardly know what to do. They often take the course of least resistance, which is to do nothing different from what they have always done. They reason that students are all alike because they are human beings; therefore, all of them should be treated the same. Or, they become susceptible to the persuasions of the conservative critics who see multicultural education as a threat to high-quality education and unity in our society.

Advocate Perspectives

Many, but by no means all, of the nationally recognized proponents of multicultural education are scholars and educators of color. Their counterparts in England, Australia, and Canada frequently align themselves with the antiracist education movement. Unlike the critics whose arguments hinge primarily on social issues, the advocates tend to focus their explanations in support of cultural pluralism and its potential for improving teaching and learning. Social benefits are important, too, but not the primary goal.

Proponents of multicultural education claim that it is, at its most fundamental level, simply an attempt to bring education closely in line with a basic characteristic of the human condition and our society: cultural, racial, ethnic, and social diversity exists! The national unity proclaimed in statements like "one nation indivisible, with liberty and justice for all" and *e pluribus unum* is still more of a vision than a reality. As Barber (1992) explained, diversity is, at once, a prominent virtue, a source of pride, a brave boast, a troubling reality, and an unsettling problem that complicates and muddles what it means culturally to be an American and a citizen of the United States. Banks (1993, 23) added that while the United States may be one nation politically, socially it is deeply divided along racial, ethnic, class, and gender lines: "Multicultural education is designed to help unify a deeply divided nation rather than to divide a highly cohesive one." It supports the national ideal of *e pluribus unum* but demands that the standard of *unum* be changed from the current Eurocentric dominance to a composite or confluence of ethnic and cultural pluralism. This new standard for creating national unity out of diversity is what Asante (1991–92) envisioned as "pluralism without hierarchy."

Asante's (1991; 1991–92) nonhierarchical, equal-status approach to education challenges the notion that because European-based culture is the majority one in the United States, it is inherently superior and universally correct and should be imposed upon other groups. Multicultural education celebrates the rich tapestry of all the peoples, cultures, and traditions that comprise the United States by studying the heritages and contributions of people of color, the poor, and females along with those of European-Americans, the middle class, and males. In this regard, multicultural education works to "close the gap between the Western democratic ideals of equality and justice and societal practices that contradict those ideals, such as discrimination based on race, gender, and social class" (Banks 1991–92, 32). Virtually all proponents of multicultural education endorse this approach to the study of ethnic, social, and cultural diversity.

The declaration that there is "no one model American" made more than 20 years ago by the American Association of Colleges for Teacher Education (AACTE) (1973) is a central theme in multicultural education and one of the two major arguments in favor of including information about different ethnic and cultural groups in school curricula and diversifying instructional strategies to accommodate a variety of ethnic and cultural learning styles. The other argument is the indisputable fact that no two human beings are totally identical. According to Butts (1978, 375) the incredibly wide variety of peoples, cultures, and experiences that comprise humankind are "the essential ingredients of both democracy and personal development." Since educational systems are integral parts and reflections of the societies in which they exist, and U.S. society is composed of so much diversity, there is no choice but for its schools to be culturally pluralistic. Therefore, multicultural education is a viable way for schools to fulfill their functions of socializing students into the national culture and providing them with the very best education possible.

Multiculturalists believe that knowing, appreciating, and participating in different cultures will lead students to agree with Martin Luther King, Jr., that "We are caught in an inescapable network of mutuality; tied in a single garment of destiny. Whatever affects one directly, affects all indirectly" (in Washington 1986, 210). Furthermore, these reciprocal interactions enrich individuals and society, make life more interesting, stimulating, and exciting; and provide more solutions to social and personal problems than are possible in monocultural systems (AACTE 1973; Pai 1984).

Multicultural education's goals for schools are not radically different from those embedded in the ideals of U.S. democratic values. But, multicultural education asks that they be reinterpreted within the context of cultural diversity. Multicultural education demands that schools "expand their concepts of political and cultural democracy to include large groups of students who have been historically denied opportunities to fully realize American democratic values and ideals" (Banks 1984, 63). Asante (1991–92) proposed achieving this expansion by "centering" children in their own cultural traditions in order to make the educational process more effective for culturally diverse students.

Asante explained that genuine "centric" education provides to African-American, Asian-American, Latino, and Native American children similar kinds of learning opportunities and experiences that are provided for European-American children: to know their own cultures, to learn in styles that are familiar to them, and to attend school in settings that celebrate their heritages. This is reasonable since "children who are centered in their own cultural information are better students, more disciplined, and have greater motivation for schoolwork" (Asante 1991–92, 30). The use of cultural examples from different ethnic groups in teaching and learning enrich the educational experiences of all students.

Critics are correct when they say that multiculturalists place a heavy emphasis on cultural understanding within and among racial, ethnic, and social groups. But, they are wrong in contending that these emphases concentrate on cultural trivia and exoticism. Proponents of multicultural education advocate comprehensive analyses of the cultural heritages of diverse ethnic groups. However, sometimes multicultural practices are not consistent with theoretical ideals and focus too much attention on obvious and superficial symbols, artifacts, customs, and traditions of cultures. Critics often emphasize this in their opposition.

However, both critics and advocates of multicultural education seem to forget the lag between educational theory and practice and the difficulties associated with implementing educational innovations. Implementation involves: a complex interplay of teacher beliefs, knowledge, experiences, and skills; the availability of leadership, curriculum, and resources; the school and community context; the existence of a supportive infrastructure; and a plethora of daily demands and constraints of operating classrooms. Often when philosophical ideals are filtered through these "reality screens," the results are less than the vision constructed in theory. The situation is complicated further by the fact that educators are frequently placed in situations where they are expected to implement multicultural education without having had adequate professional preparation and training.

Multicultural advocates believe that the cultural heritages of ethnic groups in the United States are not mutually exclusive or irreconcilable. Rather, they are closely interrelated and enriching of each other. One simple but significant indication of this belief is the way that multiculturalists routinely identify their various constituent groups. They consistently evoke their dual identities, referring to them as Mexican-Americans, Japanese-Americans, African-Americans, Chinese-Americans, Italian-Americans, and so on, rather than as Mexican, Japanese, Chinese, African, and Italian. This is revealing testimony to their commitment to *cultural dualism*—to *pluribus* and *unum,* to unity *and* diversity, to differences *and* similarities among and within ethnic and cultural groups. It personifies the belief of multiculturalists that the cultural heritages and experiences of different ethnic and social groups are legitimate and valid, and that they enhance rather than diminish individuals and society.

Sigel (1991, 7) explained further that these "cultural pluralists envision an organic relationship in which the individual freely partakes of his or her own distinctive heritage, but also becomes an integral part of the history and experience of the common culture." The position statement of the Association for Supervision and Curriculum Development Multicultural Education Commission included a similar argument, explaining that multicultural education:

> *recognizes the right of different cultures to exist, as*
> *separate and distinct entities, and acknowledges their*
> *contribution to the societal entity. It evolves from funda-*
> *mental understandings of the interaction of divergent*
> *cultures within the culture of the United States* (ASCD
> 1977, 3).

Others, such as Darder (1991), Banks (1988), and Ramirez and Castañeda (1974), referred to teaching students skills needed to function in the national culture and different ethnic cultures simultaneously as helping students become *bicultural*. All of these emphases belie the contentions of critics that multicultural education opposes national identity, loyalty, and culture.

Multicultural education rejects the notion that our cultural standard and source of knowledge is universal and absolute. Instead, it promotes an ethos of critical analysis that subjects all canons of knowledge to thoughtful and thorough interrogation. These orientations embody the features of critical inquiry that Barber (1992) described. He explained that any version of U.S. history, culture, and development that cannot withstand sharp interrogation is worthless. To question whether the history, culture, and life of the United States include sufficient and appropriate representations of the contributions of descendants of Africans, Native Americans, Asians, Pacific Islanders, Latinos, Jews, and Pakistanis does not mean that those of Europeans will be automatically denigrated or rejected. Nor does it mean that one or some of these groups will be indiscriminately glorified. Rather, all groups' contributions should be carefully scrutinized in order to gain greater knowledge of the human genius and to present a more balanced and accurate rendition of the story of the United States (Hilliard 1991–92).

Advocates also contend that multicultural education is simply "good education" for students living in an ethnically, culturally, and racially pluralistic society. On this point Suzuki (1979, 50) explained that multicultural education "basically amounts to sound educational practice coupled with a vision for a better society." It has all of the elements that constitute principles of good pedagogy, such as relevance, developmental and contextual appropriateness, validity, significance of instruction, and teaching the whole child. Additionally, it places these ideas within the context of a wider range of social and individual diversities than do traditional educational programs and practices. Multicultural education visualizes an interactive, reciprocal, and full partnership between components of cultural diversity and principles of good quality teaching. Out of this relationship emerges an educational environment where more students are actively and intellectually engaged in the learning process and are empowered through self-knowledge, affirmation, and high levels of academic achievement.

As "education for freedom," multiculturalism works to liberate individuals, groups, and society from the shackles of oppression, exploitation, and ethnocentrism. This is done by developing a moral, ethical, and political commitment to individual, group, and cultural equality; developing skills needed to function well in multicultural settings; and promoting democratic living within and among culturally pluralistic groups and communities. Parekh (1986, 26–27) explained this perspective of multicultural education as:

> an attempt to release a child from the confines of the
> ethnocentric straitjacket and to awaken him to the
> existence of other cultures, societies and ways of life and

> *thought. It is intended to de-condition the child as much*
> *as possible in order that he can go out into the world as*
> *free from biases and prejudices as possible and able and*
> *willing to explore its rich diversity. . . . Multi-cultural*
> *education is therefore not a departure from, nor incom-*
> *patible with, but a further refinement of, the liberal idea of*
> *education. It does not cut off a child from his own culture;*
> *rather it enables him to enrich, refine and take a broader*
> *view of it without losing his roots in it.*

These notions of multicultural education are a natural complement to other conceptions of it as a means of including cultural diversity in school curricula or of giving voice to diverse peoples so that they can tell their own stories. All of these are important dimensions of the freedom, equality, empowerment, inclusion, and justice of culturally diverse people in the United States to which multicultural education is committed.

Principles of Multicultural Education

The multicultural education principles included here emerged from two sources: the general education principles identified in Chapter 1 restated to fit within the framework of cultural pluralism; and the values and beliefs about the importance of including the cultures, experiences, contributions, and perspectives of different ethnic, racial, cultural, and social groups in school programs and practices. Chapters 3 to 5 examine how general education principles can be "multiculturalized" or modified for a culturally pluralistic framework. Six examples are presented here to illustrate what the "translations" will look like. They will alert you to the complementary relationships between general and multicultural education that are developed in Chapters 3 to 5.

You might "pretest" your understanding of the discussions to come by trying some "translations" of your own. Space is provided in Chart 2.1 for this exercise. See if you can create four examples. A review of the ideas discussed in Chapter 1 may be helpful in completing this task. Below are some questions to ask about your efforts to "multiculturalize" general education principles (positive answers to them mean that your efforts are successful): Do the

Chart 2.1

Multicultural Translation of General Educational Principles	
General Education	**Multicultural Education**
1. Teachers should build upon and expand the learning potential and style preferences of students.	Teaching styles should match the learning styles of different ethnic individual and cultural groups.
2. Education should facilitate the self-acceptance of students.	Education should help students accept their ethnicity as an essential component of their personal development.
3. Education is necessary for social consciousness, democratic citizenship, and personal well-being.	Knowledge about cultural, racial, and ethnic diversity is needed for citizenship in a democratic and pluralistic society.
4. Education should promote intolerance for all forms of discrimination and oppression.	Students should be taught an ethic of social justice for culturally diverse groups and individuals.
5. Relevant teaching methods and materials increase learning.	Multicultural content, experiences, and perspectives improve learning for culturally different students.
6. Education should transmit the cumulative knowledge of humankind.	Students should learn about the contributions that diverse groups and individuals have made to humankind and culture in the United States.
7.	
8.	
9.	
10.	

translations incorporate culturally pluralistic values? Do they encompass elements of both general education and multicultural education? Are the translations inclusive of many different ethnic groups, including European-Americans and groups of color? Do the translations place general educational ideas and values into multicultural contexts?

Multicultural education provides a specific context, arena, or point of reference for general education ideals applied to particular constituent groups. However, their essential meanings remain the same. To illustrate: Multicultural education may translate the general idea that "students learn more easily from materials that validate their personal experiences" into "instructional materials that present positive views of different ethnic and social groups increase the learning of students who are members of those groups." This content and context relationship is similar to those that exist between universal and particular, ideal and reality, abstract and concrete, and theory and practice.

Efforts to translate commonly held beliefs about teaching and learning into the context of specific groups' cultural orientations, life experiences, and social conditions are often stymied because many educators either do not understand or do not see the validity of the multicultural screens. They assume that when general educational principles are screened through the lens of cultural diversity, their meaning is destroyed. A case in point is the confusion surrounding multicultural educators' proposals that culturally sensitive instructional techniques be used to achieve common learning outcomes for ethnically different students. This appeal is often misunderstood as either discriminating against or lowering academic standards for Latino, African-American, Asian-American, and Native American students. Quite the contrary is true. Students from diverse backgrounds who have different learning styles require variety in teaching techniques to master the same academic skills at similar levels of proficiency. Understanding the relationship between general and multicultural education can help prevent such confusion and can help educators find ways to improve the quality of education for all students. This need grows in importance as the population in U.S. schools and society becomes more ethnically, racially, culturally, socially, and linguistically pluralistic.

In addition to sharing the principles of general education, multicultural education espouses some unique principles that emerged from a review of its leading proponents' publications. Most writings on multicultural education are pedagogical; they deal with issues and techniques of teaching and learning. Consequently, they are not easily separated into categories such as educational psychology, sociology, and philosophy; they tend to incorporate elements of all of these. The educational principles that emerge from these writings reflect this synthesis. The multicultural writings reviewed were chosen in the same way, and for similar purposes, as those about general education. They are highly selective, and illustrate how leaders in the field conceptualize educational values, content, and processes related to ethnic and cultural diversity.

The review of multicultural education scholarship revealed four categories of values and beliefs about the role of cultural pluralism in U.S. education:

1. Cultural background and ethnic identity are critical determinants of human attitudes, values, and behaviors in all settings, including teaching and learning.
2. Racial, cultural, and ethnic biases permeate schools and society, and thereby minimize individual and social potential.
3. The diversity that characterizes individuals and cultural groups requires a plurality of instructional programs and strategies, if education is to be most effective for all students.
4. The ethnic identity and cultural backgrounds of students are as important as their physical, psychological, and intellectual capabilities in planning and implementing effective educational programs.

The observations of Pai (1984), Novak (1975), Kimball (1978), and Hall (1977) illustrate the significance of culture in teaching and learning. Pai explained that because culture is so much a part of what people say and do, for educators to ignore, demean, or reject its influence on student behaviors constitutes an act of psychological and moral violence. To legitimize the significance of only one cultural system (as is most often the case in U.S. schools when only the Eurocentric mainstream culture is studied and valued) is to engage in cultural hegemony. Novak and Hall suggested that culture determines our thoughts, actions, emotions, and values and creates the standards of acceptability for all of these. According to Kimball, cultural perspectives and experiences provide the screens through which human potential is filtered, interpreted, and made meaningful.

Mason (1960) offered excellent advice to teachers: referring to the critical role of culture in the educational process, he noted that since society's values, traditions, and controls influence the personalities of its members, the best way to understand individuals is to study the societies and cultures in which they live. Furthermore, culture is a powerful medium through which teaching and learning are mediated. Educators who understand the cultures of diverse students are likely to be more successful in teaching them than those who do not make the effort to understand.

Other educators, such as Shade (1989), Boykin (1986), Ramirez and Castañeda, (1974), and Darder (1991), suggest that many individuals from different cultural, racial, ethnic, and social groups are bi- or even tricultural. If teachers are to understand the cultures and personalities of these students, they need to become familiar with their *primordial* backgrounds. They cannot assume that African-American, Asian-American, Latino, and Native American students have no culture other than the one they share with mainstream society. Social class, nationality, gender, language, and length of residence in the United States are other key factors that influence how the "raw materials" of culture are applied and expressed in human behavior. Teachers must understand how all of these affect the personalities and potential of their students.

Schools have cultures, too, and the educational processes they use are culturally determined. Students and teachers bring all of their cultural experiences, perspectives, and screens to the classroom with them. Often these cultures conflict with each other, and learning suffers. This point was explained cogently by Spindler (1987) and his associates; they concluded that the greater the extent to which there is cultural incompatibility among students, teachers, methods, materials, values, and expectations, the more likely the educational process will be less successful for everyone. Several researchers, including Boggs, Watson-Gegeo and McMillen (1985), Boykin (1982), Cazden, John, and Hymes (1985), and Greenbaum (1985), found this to be the case with Native Hawaiian, Native American, Latino, and African-American students. These findings suggest that the emphasis multicultural education places on matching the home cultural styles of diverse students with those of the school is a viable way to improve the quality of their learning.

Another argument that multiculturalists use as a basis for generating and justifying principles of education for cultural diversity is the effect of what Cortés (1991) and Gollnick and Chinn (1990) called the "societal curriculum"— the attitudes, values, and images of culturally different groups portrayed in popular culture and transmitted to schools. Unfortunately, most of these continue to be negative and stereotypical. Even though they may be more subtle than blatant, more benign than malicious, and more incidental than intentional, the negative consequences are nonetheless devastating. For example, the image left by prime-time television programs and advertising is that only Anglo-Americans and African-Americans live in the United States since they are most often the only groups portrayed. African-Americans who appear as regulars in programs that are not predominantly Black rarely are involved in *sustained and stable* family and intimate relationships. The subtle message is that these do not exist in real life.

A closely related image and frequently used metaphor for African-American males that appears in popular culture and academic scholarship is "an endangered species." No other group is referred to by a designation usually reserved for animals. Descriptions and role functions of Native Americans are translated into negative stereotypic images and used as mascots for high school, college, and professional athletic teams. Thus, sports news tells about the feats and failures of the Braves, Chiefs, Indians, Warriors, and Redskins. Automobile manufacturers get into the act by giving tribal names to their products such as the Navaho truck and Cherokee jeep. In other instances, groups of color, the poor, females, and other ethnic minorities are not represented at all. These oversights are especially prominent in those formal structures of society that have high social and power status such as law, politics, and business. Cultural, ethnic, and racial diversity are far more evident in other areas of society that are popular but of relatively low status with respect to power and influence in shaping policy (such as the food, fashion, entertainment, sports, and tourism industries).

Schools mirror these trends, and thereby perpetuate social class, racial, gender, and cultural inequities in several ways. One is relegating the teaching of cultural diversity and multicultural education to special events, celebrations and ceremonies, and to what some people consider low-status, "low capital value" subject areas, such as social studies, literature, humanities, and the fine arts. Another is the overrepresentation of African-Americans, Latinos, Native

Americans, and poor students in low-level curriculum tracks (i.e., general education as opposed to college prep or office and secretarial preparation instead of business management), low-status courses (general math versus algebra or calculus), vocational education, and special education. A third discriminatory practice is the continued use of standardized test scores to assign students to gifted, talented, and Advanced Placement (AP) courses despite evidence gathered over a long period of time that shows most groups of color and students of lower socioeconomic status score significantly lower than their Anglo and middle-class counterparts. The only deviation from this pattern occurs with Japanese-, Chinese-, and Korean-Americans whose test scores are comparable to European-Americans in most academic areas tested. However, they do not score as well on tests measuring social, communicative, and interpersonal relations.

Practices like these create an academic caste system in which Latinos, African-Americans, Native Americans, and females are repeatedly disadvantaged, and European-Americans (especially males) are consistently advantaged. They violate principles of equality and justice in the rules, structures, and procedures of schooling that regulate the quality and distribution of learning opportunities. These practices are analogous to the employment of disproportionate numbers of individuals of color and poverty in minimum wage, entry level, and unskilled jobs in society.

Imani Perry (1988), a fifteen-year-old African-American student, reflecting on her experiences in public and private schools, offered poignant personal observations about the kind of academic discrimination experienced in schools even by achieving students of color. She described transferring from an upper-class private school, where she was one of the few minority students, into upper-level classes in a multiracial school where she continued to be "one of the very few." In the public school, she observed and experienced a kind of teaching that emphasized form, formulas, facts, and behavior instead of learning significant knowledge, exploring ideas, thinking critically and analytically, and being creative. Well-behaved meant "always taking the teacher's word as absolute truth and never questioning the teacher's authority. This definition of well-behaved is of course culturally based and can be in opposition to cultures of Black and Hispanic students" (Perry 1988, 335). Perry concluded that this neglect of intellectual development, based on teachers' assumptions that students of color are less intelligent, fails to establish cultur-ally sensitive relationships between students and teachers, and trains students for low-powered and menial jobs.

These practices were especially prevalent with African-American, Latino, and Native American students who retained strong ethnic identities and cultural characteristics. Several authors have written detailed descriptions of various aspects of groups' cultures that conflict with the normative values, rules, and structures of schools, which Gay (1991) summarized.

The higher incidence of disciplinary referrals for Latinos and African-Americans means that they are removed from the instructional process more often than other students. School rules enforced more rigorously for certain students aggravate racial tensions and hostilities and raise questions about racial inequities. One such case occurred in a high school in Anchorage, Alaska. While visiting this school, I learned that the African-American students (mostly male) were irate about being punished for "hanging on the wall." They could not understand why the principal established a rule that prohibited students from congregating in a particular hallway before and after school. According to them, they were not rowdy, loud, or causing any trouble. This was just a place to gather and visit with friends. The students felt the rule was particularly unfair to African-Americans, since the school had established for other ethnic groups (such as the Native Alaskans and Latinos) a place and time to meet. No similar provisions were made for African-Americans, so they began "hanging on the wall."

The frequent and pervasive occurrence of these kinds of academic and disciplinary discriminatory practices in schools provide multiculturalists with persuasive reasons for the principles they offer. Suggestions for promoting cultural equity, ensuring equal access to high-status knowledge for all stu-dents, teaching students to become social change agents, and developing an ethic of human dignity and social justice come directly from these "societal and symbolic curricula." All students, not just those who are poor and from groups of color, are victimized by ethnic and social class bias in curriculum content, by the failure to learn skills for cross-cultural interactions, and by not understanding how the lives of ethnic individuals and groups in the United States are closely interrelated. Therefore, multicultural education should be infused throughout the entire curricula of all schools (Suzuki 1984). Furthermore, eliminating discrimination and providing for equity in the educational process require comprehensive and complex efforts throughout the infrastructure of the schooling system (Banks and Banks 1993). This is why proponents of multicultural education believe that systemic institutional change is necessary to ensure the full participation of culturally diverse groups is fundamental to the effective implementation of multicultural education and reform of society.

From these values and beliefs emerge several principles of multicultural education that reinforce and extend the ones shared with general education. They are grounded in the concepts of cultural equality, cultural compatibility, education as a cultural process, and reciprocity between cultural equity and educational excellence. These principles are summarized in Table 2.1 below. In the remaining chapters they are integrated with discussions of the relationship between general and multicultural education.

Table 2.1

Specific Principles of Multicultural Education
◆ Multicultural education is appropriate for all students, subjects, grades, and school settings.
◆ Cultural diversity is a normal trait of our society and humankind; cultural pluralism, therefore, should occur routinely in the educational process in order to accommodate and value diversity.
◆ The close interactive relationship between culture, ethnicity, and learning validates the need for multicultural education.
◆ Multicultural education is a valuable and valid tool for achieving educational access, equity, relevance, and excellence for culturally different students.
◆ Teaching culturally different students is more effective when it is culturally contextualized.
◆ Education should promote cultural diversity in the United States without hierarchy, imperialism, or hegemony.
◆ Understanding and accepting cultural diversity are fundamental to building social and political unity among diverse racial, ethnic, and social groups.
◆ Educational equity and excellence are reciprocally related; the achievement of one is a condition of the other.
◆ Multicultural education empowers individuals and groups for personal liberation and social transformation.
◆ Cultural diversity should be infused throughout all aspects of the educational process.

Reflections and Applications

The arguments for and against multicultural education presented in this chapter are selective and illustrative. Many other individuals and perspectives on each side of the debate could be included. However, those mentioned represent the major dimensions of the debate about the relationship between the visions of multicultural and general education. They deal with three key issues—establishing the primary goals of education, promoting social cohesion and national unity, and determining the most effective methods of teaching and learning. The critics tend to focus on the *social* consequences of multicultural education. They contend that the emphasis it places on differences among ethnic, social, and cultural groups creates obstacles to racial harmony, national unity, and promotion of the common good across groups. Beyond responding to the claims of critics, proponents of multicultural education concentrate on its *pedagogical* potential. They believe it can make the educational process more relevant and effective academically, socially, and psychologically for *all* students—European-Americans and groups of color; immigrants and citizens; females and males; poor and middle class; urban, rural, and suburban; elementary, secondary, and college. Multicultural education is also essential if schools are to fulfill their basic function of socializing students for the society in which they live.

Advocates of multicultural education view it as a means of helping the educational process reflect social realities, enriching the common national culture, and ensuring that all students have the right to freedom, justice, dignity, and unrestricted participation in all dimensions of the educational process. It is also a means of promoting cultural equality, equity, and excellence in school programs and practices. Therefore, proponents of multicultural education view it as a restatement, translation, or application of the democratic principles to which our society and schools are committed *within the context of ethnic and cultural pluralism.*

Two underlying premises of this book are worth mentioning here since they serve as a *conceptual bridge* between the first two chapters and the last three. First, knowledge is enlightening and empowering. Educators can make better choices and decisions about multicultural education practices in classrooms when they have a thorough understanding of the field. Knowledge about the various philosophical arguments in the debate over multicultural education helps teachers better understand why certain strategies are suggested and by whom. It is a good guide for helping educators maneuver through the maze of suggestions offered about why multicultural education is important and how it should be implemented, and finding those that are compatible with their own needs, values, beliefs, goals, skills, and teaching contexts.

The second underlying premise is that demonstrating how general and multicultural education principles are closely related can create a "connecting bridge" across the schism between advocates and critics, theory and practice, ideals and realities. The debate over multicultural education is fueled by basic differences in value priorities of the critics and advocates and tensions between forces for change and maintaining the status quo. However, some of the disagreement is due to miscommunication on both sides and the tendency of critics to assume that the philosophy and beliefs of the advocate scholars are synonymous with classroom practices. It is important for all educators to remember that while values, beliefs, and ideals have a significant influence on practice, theory and practice are never identical. The ideas presented in this chapter about the debate over the nature, purposes, functions, and benefits of multicultural education should help educators avoid these pitfalls in future discussions about multicultural principles and practices, and thereby improve the quality of both.

Six suggestions are offered here to extend and further clarify your understanding of the ideas discussed in this chapter.

1. Now that you have had a chance to read some of the major arguments for and against multicultural education, write a reflective essay on the controversial debate surrounding multicultural education. Address such questions as: What do you feel are the most sensitive points of contention of each side of the debate (in your own words)? How do these points of view compare with your own? With which of the critics or advocates mentioned in the chapter do you feel a personal affinity or strong sense of shared vision? Do you think that there can ever be a meeting of the minds between the advocates and critics of multicultural education? How might this be achieved and to what benefit? After you have identified the person in the debate with whom you have a strong affinity, you may want to read the complete text of some of his or her writings to further clarify your personal position on multicultural education.

2. Find examples of the conflicting arguments about multicultural education. Working in conjunction with members of your instructional department, teaching team, a study group, or other interested colleagues, examine your school's formal and informal curricula, social climate, and interpersonal relations to see if you can locate illustrations of some of the specific points made by the critics and the advocates. For example, is there any indication of hostility among students from different racial groups, or has the resistance of teachers increased or decreased as a result of introducing multicultural education in your school? If you find evidence of increased hostility, develop a position statement explaining why this occurred, selecting from the arguments presented in this chapter. Include some suggestions for how this hostility can be alleviated. If you find decreased hostility, ask students, teachers, and administrators what accounted for this. Compare their responses and categorize them according to the different explanations about the benefits of multicultural education that are offered by its proponents. If your search reveals that currently there are no multicultural education practices being implemented, develop a list of recommendations for your school to undertake. These should reflect your own personal beliefs or those implied by the advocacy arguments presented in this chapter. They might include suggestions for curriculum changes, instructional strategies, media materials, a selected list of readings on multicultural education for the professional staff, or examples of visual images that convey multicultural education ideals.

3. Conduct an informal survey of your colleagues. Ask them to share their opinions about the meaning, potential problems, and benefits of multicultural education. Group these into categories according to the kinds of arguments presented in this chapter. For instance, list ideas for improving access to high-quality educational opportunities for students of color and the benefits of multicultural education for European-American students. Compare your survey results with the arguments presented in this chapter. Use the comments collected in your survey to determine which perspectives on multicultural education are most prominent among your colleagues. Then, write an "institutional position statement" on multicultural education for your school, using comments you selected from the survey. This statement may criticize multicultural education principles or advocate them.

4. If you still have questions about the arguments for and against multicultural education, consider reading some primary sources on the issue. The works by Schlesinger (1992) and Ravitch (1990), cited in the reference list on page 61, present critical viewpoints. Two useful references for the advocacy position are Banks (1993) and Suzuki (1984).

5. Analyze a multicultural education program that has been in the center of the debate about issues of educational quality. Two possibilities are the New York State Department of Education's 1989 Curriculum of Inclusion and the 1987 California History-Social Science Framework. Examine one of these carefully, or compare the two to identify ideas that might be highly contentious. Use the discussion in this chapter as a point of reference to explain why and how these parts of the proposal can be attacked by critics and, simultaneously, applauded by proponents of multicultural education. You might also compare your analyses with some of those that have been conducted by other educators. To obtain a copy of the Curriculum of Inclusion write to:

> Office of the Commissioner
> Room 115 Education Building
> New York State Education Department
> Albany, NY 12234

The California History-Social Science Framework can be obtained from:

> California State Department of Education
> Bureau of Publications Sales
> P. O. Box 271
> Sacramento, CA 95802-0271

6. Work with your students or colleagues to conduct a "content analysis" of a popular newsmagazine's treatment of the increasing diversity of U.S. society and schools over a specified period of time, perhaps three or five years. Select articles in which diversity was highlighted, from two or three issues of the magazine in each year of your selected time frame. When analyzing the content of the articles, ask questions such as:

- What factual aspects of ethnic and cultural diversity were emphasized?
- What were the major themes or messages of the article?
- What was the overall tone of the article (e.g., advocacy, critique, celebration, anxiety, etc.)?

- Were there any shifts in the tone and emphases of the coverage across the years of analysis?

- How do these articles contradict, validate, complement, and/or illustrate the issues, ideas, and arguments presented in this chapter?

- What are the implications for educational and social action relative to cultural diversity?

References

American Association of Colleges for Teacher Education (AACTE). 1973. *No one model American.* Washington, D.C.: AACTE.

Asante, M. K. 1991. The Afrocentric idea in education. *Journal of Negro Education* 60: 170–80.

Asante, M. K. 1991–92. Afrocentric curriculum. *Educational Leadership* 49: 28–31.

Association for Supervision and Curriculum Development (ASCD) Multicultural Education Commission. 1977. Encouraging multicultural education. In *Multicultural education: Commitments, issues, and applications,* ed. C. A. Grant, 1–5. Washington, D.C.: ASCD.

Banks, J. A. 1984. Multicultural education and its critics: Britain and the United States. *The New Era* 65: 58–65.

Banks, J. A. 1988. *Multiethnic education: Theory and practice.* Boston: Allyn and Bacon.

Banks, J. A. 1991–92. Multicultural education: For freedom's sake. *Educational Leadership* 49(4): 32–36.

Banks, J. A. 1993. Multicultural education: Developments, dimensions, and challenges. *Phi Delta Kappan* 75: 22–28.

Banks, J. A. 1994. *An introduction to multicultural education.* Boston: Allyn and Bacon.

Banks, J. A., and C. A. M. Banks, eds. 1993. *Multicultural education: Issues and perspectives.* Boston: Allyn and Bacon.

Barber, B. R. 1992. *An aristocracy for everyone: The politics of education and the future of America.* New York: Ballantine Books.

Boggs, S. T., K. Watson-Gegeo, and G. McMillen. 1985. *Speaking, relating, and learning: A study of Hawaiian children at home and at school.* Norwood: Ablex.

Boykin, A. W. 1982. Task variability and the performance of black and white students: Vervistic explorations. *Journal of Black Studies* 12: 469–85.

Boykin, A. W. 1986. The triple quandary and the schooling of Afro-American children. In *The school achievement of minority children: New perspectives,* ed. U. Neisser, 57–92. Hillsdale, N.J.: Lawrence Erlbaum.

Bullivant, B. M. 1984. *Pluralism: Cultural maintenance and evolution.* Clevedon, England: Multilingual Matters.

Chapter 2

Bullivant, B. M. 1986. Towards radical multiculturalism: Resolving tensions in curriculum and educational planning. In *Multicultural education: The interminable debate*, ed. S. Modgil, G. K. Verma, K. Mallick, and C. Modgil, 133–47. London: Falmer Press.

Butts, R. F. 1978. *Public education in the United States: From revolution to reform*. New York: Holt, Rinehart and Winston.

Cazden, C. B., V. P. John, and D. Hymes, eds. 1985. *Functions of language in the classroom*. New York: Teachers College.

Cole, M. 1992. British values, liberal values, or values of justice and equality: Three approaches to education in multicultural Britain. In *Equity or excellence? Education and cultural reproduction. Cultural diversity and the schools,* vol. 3, ed. J. Lynch, C. Modgil, and S. Modgil, 239–63. London: Falmer Press.

Cortés, C. E. 1991. Empowerment through media literacy: A multicultural approach. In *Empowerment through multicultural education,* ed. C. E. Sleeter, 43–157. Albany: State University of New York Press.

Darder, A. 1991. *Culture and power in the classroom: A critical foundation for bicultural education*. New York: Bergin and Garvey.

Davidman, L. and P. T. Davidman. 1994. *Teaching with a multicultural perspective: A practical guide*. New York: Longman.

D'Souza, D. 1991. *Illiberal education: The politics of race and sex on campus*. New York: Free Press.

Gay, G. 1991. Culturally diverse students and social studies. In *Handbook of research on social studies teaching and learning,* ed. J. P. Shaver, 144–56. New York: Macmillan.

Gollnick, D. M., and P. C. Chinn, eds. 1990. *Multicultural education in a pluralistic society*. Columbus, Ohio: Merrill.

Greenbaum, P. E. 1985. Nonverbal differences in communication style between American Indian and Anglo elementary classrooms. *American Educational Journal* 22: 101–15.

Hall, E. T. 1979. *Beyond culture*. Garden City, N.Y.: Anchor Press.

Henry, W, III. 1990. Beyond the melting pot. *Time* (April 9) 135: 28–31.

Hilliard, A. G., III. 1991–92. Why we must pluralize the curriculum. *Educational Leadership* 49: 12–14.

Howard, G. R. 1993. Whites in multicultural education: Rethinking our role. *Phi Delta Kappan* 75: 36–41.

Kimball, S. T. 1978. The transmission of culture. In *Schooling in the cultural context: Anthropological studies of education,* ed. J. I. Roberts and S. K. Akinsanya, 57–271. New York: McKay.

Leicester, M. 1992. Antiracism versus the new multiculturalism: Moving beyond the interminable debate. In *Equity or excellence? Education and cultural reproduction. Cultural diversity and the schools,* vol. 3, ed. J. Lynch, C. Modgil, and S. Modgil, 215–29. London: Falmer Press.

Mason, R.E. 1960. *Educational ideals in American society*. Boston: Allyn and Bacon.

McCarthy, C. 1988. Rethinking liberal and radical perspectives on racial inequality in schooling: Making the case for nonsynchrony. *Harvard Educational Review* 58: 265–79.

Mullard, C. 1984. *Anti-racist education The three O's.* Cardiff: National Association for Multiracial Education.

Novak, M. 1975. Variety is more than a slice of life. *Momentum* 6: 24–27.

Ogbu, J. U. 1991. Immigrant and involuntary minorities in comparative perspective. In *Equity or excellence? Education and cultural reproduction. Cultural diversity and the schools,* vol. 3, ed. M. A. Gibson and J. U. Ogbu, 3–33. New York: Garland Publishing.

Ogbu, J. U. 1992. Understanding cultural diversity and learning. *Educational Researcher* 21: 5–14, 24.

Pai, Y. 1984. Cultural diversity and multicultural education. *Lifelong Learning* 7: 7–9, 27.

Parekh, B. 1986. The concept of multi-cultural education. In *Multicultural education: The interminable debate,* ed. S. Modgil, G. K. Verma, K. Mallick, and C. Modgil, 19–31. London: Falmer Press.

Perry, I. 1988. A black student's reflection on public and private schools. *Harvard Educational Review* 58: 332–36.

Ramirez, M., and A. Castañeda. 1974. *Cultural democracy: Bicognitive development and education.* New York: Academic Press.

Ravitch, D. 1990. Diversity and democracy: Multicultural education in America. *American Educator* 14: 16–20, 46–48.

Schlesinger, A. M., Jr. 1992. *The disuniting of America: Reflections on a multicultural society.* New York: Norton.

Shade, B. J., ed. 1989. *Culture, style, and the educative process.* Springfield, Ill.: Charles C. Thomas Publishers.

Sigel, R. S. 1991. Democracy in the multi-ethnic society. In *Education for democratic citizenship: A challenge for multiethnic societies,* ed. R. S. Sigel and M. B. Hoskin, 3–8. Hillsdale, N.J.: Lawrence Erlbaum Associates.

Spindler, G. D., ed. 1987. *Education and cultural process: Anthropological approaches.* Prospect Heights, Ill.: Waveland Press.

Suzuki, B. H. 1984. Curriculum transformation for multicultural education. *Education and Urban Society* 16: 294–322.

Suzuki, B. H. 1979. Multicultural education: What's it all about? *Integrate Education* 12: 43–49.

Taba, H. 1962. *Curriculum development: Theory and practice.* New York: Harcourt, Brace and World.

Troyna, B. 1987. Beyond multiculturalism: Towards the enactment of anti-racist education in policy, provision and pedagogy. *Oxford Review of Education* 13: 307–20.

Washington, J. M., ed. 1986. *A testament of hope: The essential writings of Martin Luther King, Jr.* New York: Harper and Row.

Chapter 3

Principles of Human Growth and Development

We become more enlightened about the nature of the person with his [or her] unpredictable and predictable qualities when we view him [or her] from many perspectives.

(Roderick 1977, 203)

No matter what a person's social status, material wealth, or trappings of success, if that person remains frustrated by questions of selfhood, how meaningful is his or her life?

(Hedges and Martinello 1977, 230)

Meeting the individual needs of students is of paramount importance to virtually all teachers, although the reasons given for its significance vary widely. Some explanations emphasize personal aspects of development; others focus on the social. John Dewey, well known for his support of child-centered education, wrote eloquently in the early 1900s about the central role of students in educational decision making. Many teachers are still influenced by his ideas. In *The Child and the Curriculum* (1902), he declared that the child is the beginning, center, and end reference for all decisions. Whether from the perspective of individual needs or as members of groups, the growth and development patterns of children should furnish the baseline standard and set the visionary ideal for all that is done in the name of education.

Teachers have many ways of expressing their commitment to the human development of students, especially when the issue is raised in relation to cultural diversity and multicultural education. Many declare, "When I look at my students, I see no differences. I treat them all the same." Almost simultaneously, they proclaim, "Every child is an individual human being and should be treated accordingly." Implicit in these statements is the tendency to equate social, racial, and cultural differences with inferiority and discrimination. Saying "I see no differences" is a way of declaring innocence of bias and prejudice. Multicultural education contends that the individuality and humanity of students cannot be genuinely addressed without accepting their diverse ethnic identities and cultural experiences. Race, class, ethnicity, culture, and gender are important components of humanity, and they should not be ignored or neglected in the educational development of individuals in our society.

Three other major assumptions underlie the principles of human development discussed in this chapter. First, heredity alone does not determine human potential and learning. It contributes the raw materials but does not guarantee their realization (Loree 1970). Second, "an individual becomes the kind of person he or she is as a result of continuing and continuous interaction between a growing, changing biological organism and its physical, psychological, and social environment" (Conger and Petersen 1984, 32). That is, culture and socialization are required to convert human potential into reality. The third assumption is the concept of antecedent-consequent relationships. It holds that "the effects of events occurring at any one stage of development depend on and proceed from the developmental events that preceded them and will, in turn, influence the individual's responses to future events" (Conger and Petersen 1984, 33). These assumptions have profound implications for providing effective education to all students, including developmental compatibility, comprehensiveness in curriculum and instruction, diversity of instructional methods and materials, and early and cumulative school success.

The human development concepts most frequently invoked in educational theory are continuity, sequence, and progression; critical tasks and periods in development; motivation; individual diversity and human universality; cumulative effects of experience; and maximizing personal potential. Multicultural education adds the dimension of *cultural context* to these. It contends that these principles cannot be fully understood or translated into practice for culturally different students unless they are interpreted through the screens of their diverse ethnic identities, cultural orientations, and background experiences.

This chapter attempts to place the general principles of human growth and development identified in Chapter 1 (see Table 1.1 on page 19) into the contexts of ethnic diversity and multicultural education. Principles of human growth and development and their implications for education are highly interrelated, rather than discrete and mutually exclusive. This is also true for principles of citizenship and socialization, and pedagogy (see Chapters 4 and 5). Therefore, no attempt is made to discuss separately each of the principles identified in Chapter 1. Such an attempt would be redundant. Instead, this chapter is organized according to the four major themes represented by the specific principles listed in Chapter 1. (The same technique is also used for organizing Chapters 4 and 5.) The four themes are *holistic growth, universal psychological needs and developmental tasks, identity development,* and *individuality and universality.* Each of these sections begins with abbreviated statements of the general education principles—and their multicultural translations—related to each theme.

Before reading further, complete the following activity. It will help establish a practical baseline or point of reference for the ideas discussed in this chapter about principles of human development and their implications for classroom practice. Develop an "Inventory of Personal Development Techniques." Acquire ideas for this inventory by consulting your colleagues, or observing in classrooms, or thinking back to your experiences as a student, in order to identify different techniques teachers use to acknowledge and facilitate the individual development of students. These might include use of student assistants, personal counseling in the classroom, recognizing special talents, or having peer tutors. Keep your inventory close at hand as you read this chapter, and think about how it could be modified or extended.

Holistic Growth

General Principles:	Multicultural Translations:
• Human growth is multidimensional and holistic.	• Ethnic and cultural factors are key aspects of human development.
• Human growth is sequential.	• Sequence of growth is influenced by cultural environments.
• Human growth varies in rate.	• Rate of growth is affected by cultural conditions.

Teachers use their knowledge of developmental psychology to plan the scope, sequence, and pacing of their instruction. For example, we know that all individuals go through the same stages of intellectual, social, emotional, physical, and moral development. The patterns within this normal process of human growth and development are continuous and comprehensive among and within individuals. This means that all individuals experience similar stages and sequences of growth; that the entire organism is involved in the developmental process; and that what happens at one stage of growth is a foundation for subsequent stages. For example, understanding concrete ideas is a prerequisite to abstract thinking in intellectual development. How children are socialized culturally affects how they perform intellectually. Physical changes cause emotional and social changes and are, in turn, affected by them. The advent of puberty is accompanied by anatomical changes and ethnic identity changes, and both influence the other. Abraham Maslow (1954) described these patterns of changes as being circular, interrelated, consistent, holistic, and internally stable.

However, rates of change and their specific details are not uniform or identical across individuals and groups. Not everyone experiences or ex-presses the stages of development in the same way or at the same pace. Some of this variability results from biological factors, but much of it is sociological and cultural. Simpson (1977, 188) summarized this idea: "While sharing our humanity, we differ from members of other groups around the world and through time because the groups within which we interact, while fulfilling much the same human needs, differ in values and in action." Maslow (1954) lent additional support to the importance of cultural influences on human developmental patterns. According to his research, the relationships between culture and personality are too complex and too profound to be treated lightly. How the main goals of life are achieved, how self-esteem is expressed, how status roles are determined, and what are the appropriate levels of security, sociality, and activity for individuals are largely, although not totally, culturally determined. These concepts contribute to multiculturalists' beliefs that understanding cultural differences is fundamental to appreciating individu-ality and humanity, and that race, ethnicity, culture, and social class are all major factors in the human development of individuals and deserve a place of significance in educational decision making.

Both general educators and multiculturalists agree that four sets of factors—intellectual, physical, moral, and socioemotional—need to be exam-ined in concert with each other in order to better understand the attitudes, values, and behaviors of individuals and to design corresponding develop-mentally appropriate educational programs. This is especially important for ethnically different students because their cultural backgrounds and experi-ences add another layer to general developmental characteristics. Teachers need to understand these and learn how to design educational experiences that are sensitive and responsive to cultural variations in developmental patterns. Otherwise, the Eurocentric dominance in the educational system could lead them to try to make children of color into carbon copies of middle-class Whites.

Even though European-American, Arab-American, African-American, and Vietnamese-American students may be going through puberty at the same time and may exhibit many of these changes in the same way, some behaviors have unique expression according to cultural identity. These might be observable in friendship choices, management of conflicts, body adornment, and kinds of symbols and insignias used as notations of ethnic identity. The value priorities and related socialization styles of different ethnic and cultural groups also influence how developmental patterns are shaped. Individuals from cultural groups that place relatively little emphasis on social interactions may not be as advanced in this area as their counterparts who come from cultures where this is a high priority. For example, African-Americans, whose culture prizes interpersonal interactions and verbal skills, are far more astute in verbal communication in social and informal settings than in written communication in isolated, formal environments. These value priorities can become significant points of intersection between multicultural and general education at the level of acting to improve teaching and learning for more students.

Another interpretation of holistic human development is that physical, social, mental, and emotional changes occur simultaneously. These changes are interrelated, but the resulting symphony they create is not always evenly balanced or harmonized. Children who are intellectually precocious are not necessarily socially and emotionally mature at comparable levels. Some individuals have highly developed computer and technological skills but are virtually incompetent in interpersonal relationships. Others whose academic abilities are barely adequate may be acknowledged social leaders and be emotionally mature. They may find it extremely difficult to pass any subject without a struggle yet are very charismatic and personable in social and interpersonal settings. The realization of other students' high intellectual potential may be blocked by feelings of rejection, ambivalence, shame, or dissonance associated with their ethnic and racial identity.

Fordham and Ogbu (1986) illustrated how intellectual and social development may be out of balance. Their study examined the attitudes of high school African-Americans in Washington, D.C., with respect to academic success. Although intellectually capable, the students did not perform well in school or disguised their academic success with illusions of failure. The authors concluded that these behaviors occurred because the African-American students who participated in the study tended to define academic success as a European-American prerogative; the students did not want to be accused by their ethnic peers of "acting White"; and they began to doubt their own intellectual ability after educators repeatedly refused to acknowledge or celebrate it. This is an example of how a certain kind of social and emotional development—emerging ethnic consciousness and a particular kind of related socially adaptive behavior—interfered with intellectual development. It is also an illustration of how the individual potential of culturally different students can become distorted or aborted when their ethnic identities and cultural heritages are not a valued part of school programs and practices. If the students in the Fordham and Ogbu (1986) study had thought their ethnicity was an acceptable part of their humanity to be developed in school along with their intellect, they would not have felt that one had to be sacrificed for the other. This possibility suggests that the students' attitudes and actions were not entirely wrong or irrational and contradicts Ogbu's (1992) interpretation that cultural identity is detrimental to motivation, aspiration, and achievement. From a multicultural education viewpoint, as long as the educational process ignores ethnic and cultural diversity or creates situations where some students feel that they must sacrifice their ethnicity in order to receive an education, we cannot say with any confidence that complete human development of African-Americans, other groups of color, limited English speakers, or children of poverty is occurring.

Another example of education failing to facilitate the comprehensive development of students frequently occurs with Asian-American students, especially those from Japanese, Chinese, and Korean ancestry. Students from these groups are often called the "model minority" because high percentages of them perform well on portions (mathematics and analysis) of standardized tests (National Center for Education Statistics 1993). These results fail to acknowledge that many of the same students have poor interpersonal skills and low physical and ethnic identity self-concepts.

Multicultural education argues that no individual can be declared "successful" or any group held up as a genuine "model of achievement" until *all* dimensions of human growth and development—the intellectual, emotional, social, aesthetic, ethical, moral, and physical—have reached equally high levels of accomplishment. This is one of the main reasons why advocates of multicultural education are so adamant that school policies, programs, and practices include both cultural diversity *and* academic excellence for students from all ethnic groups, social classes, and cultural backgrounds.

That individual capacity varies *within* each of the different domains (intellectual, social, moral, emotional, ethnic) of development is another fundamental that teachers accept as a guiding principle for classroom instruction. Students are not equally capable in all subjects taught or even in all aspects of a particular subject. Some may pass Spanish and set the achievement curve in calculus and history but demonstrate only mediocre performance in music. Others may find the skills necessary for reading short stories, drama, and narrative writing very easy to master but be challenged by technical writing, poetry, and grammar. Some students may find certain periods in history totally captivating and intellectually engaging, and other eras completely perplexing. Some students may be highly articulate when writing but virtually mute when called upon to express themselves orally. Youths who are highly ethnocentric may not see any contradictions between this and accusing others of being culturally prejudiced against them. They also may be very accommodating to members of their own ethnic group but extremely intolerant of "ethnic others." Holliday (1985) referred to this variability in skills according to task and setting as having "situational competence."

Universal Psychological Needs and Developmental Tasks

General Principles:	Multicultural Translations:
• Behavior is internally and externally motivated.	• Motivation varies by ethnic and cultural group, situation, and context.
• Psychological needs are hierarchical.	• Psychological needs are satisfied in culturally specific ways.

Closely related to the view of human development as a total process involving the entire organism is the idea that all individuals have certain psychological needs that must be satisfied in order for them to be healthy and fully functioning. These psychological needs and the associated developmental tasks linked with critical periods or stages in the life cycle, especially those

Self-Sufficiency

Self-Actualization
Self-Fulfillment, Development,
Creativity, Autonomy

Self-Esteem Needs
Achievement, Adequacy, Mastery, Competence,
Confidence, Reliance, Status, Recognition

Belonging Needs
Love, Affection

Safety Needs
Peacefulness; Lack of Danger, Anxiety, Fear

Physiological Needs
Food, Clothing, Shelter

Other-Dependency

Figure 3.1 Maslow's Hierarchy of Needs

As individuals advance up the scale of psychological needs, they become less other-dependent and more self-sufficient.
Source: Based on Maslow, A. H. 1954. *Motivation and Personality.* New York: Harper and Row.

that coincide with the school years. Psychological needs are usually regarded as the motivators or energizers of human behavior (Conger and Petersen 1984; Loree 1970).

Maslow's (1954) Hierarchy of Needs (see Figure 3.1) is one of the models of psychological needs most familiar to educators; however, it is not necessarily unique. There are many models that convey a similar message. These models suggest that psychological needs and tasks are cumulative and progressive. As such, some are more fundamental or basic than others, and their satisfaction is a prerequisite to the achievement of more complex, higher-order needs. They usually begin with such basic physical needs as food, clothing, and shelter and progress to psychoemotional needs, such as security, belonging, self-concept, acceptance, achievement, and competence. For Maslow (1954), the highest need and task is self-actualization, which is sometimes referred to as personal autonomy and realization. As individuals progress from satisfying physical needs toward self-actualization, they become increasingly more human and humane, happy and serene, loyal, friendly, and conscious of civic responsibility. According to Maslow (1954, 149–50), "people living at the level of self-actualization are, in fact, found simultaneously to love humankind most and to be the most developed idiosyncratically." In this schema, learning is a very high-order need and skill (Combs and Snygg 1959; Maslow 1954).

Typically, educational programs designed around developmental hierarchies of needs tend to progress from simple to complex, from concrete to abstract, from parts to whole. It is a common pattern observed in most school programs, both across grades and throughout subjects within grades. It is often called the "expanding spiral" approach to curriculum design. Its *linear* approach to organization is similar to many other ways in which mainstream culture conceptualizes and arranges space, relationships, and experiences. However, this orientation to educational planning and teaching can be problematic for ethnically different students whose cultures do not have the same perceptions of how learning experiences should be sequenced. Some cultures, such as those of Mexican-Americans, Native Hawaiians, and African-Americans, tend to arrange space and relationships in a circular fashion and to deal with complexity and simplicity simultaneously. Thus, young Mexican-American children are present and participate in adult functions along with grown-ups, instead of being separated from them. In schools these students are likely to be more *gestalt* in their approaches to learning—they want to see the "big picture" first, move sequentially from the whole to the parts, and combine cognition with emotions.

Multicultural education does not challenge or contradict any of these claims. It contends that these needs are so closely interwoven with culture and ethnicity that they cannot be understood outside of their cultural contexts. Multiculturalists also identify aspects of developmental needs that can cause major misunderstandings, and others that are particularly appropriate for culturally pluralistic sensitivities and interpretations. For example, security and belonging are considered to be prerequisite conditions and major goals to be accomplished in order to establish the best climate for learning in pluralistic classrooms. And, students feel more secure in learning environments where they see reflections of themselves in instructional materials—and where they are successful. Consequently, self-concepts of ethnic students should be developed in tandem with academic and subject matter skills.

By the time many racially, ethnically, culturally, and socially different children begin their formal education, they already have internalized the negative values attached to their groups and cultures by racist and ethnocentric forces in mainstream society. They arrive at school only to discover that there is little of significance about their groups' heritages, cultures, and contributions in the content and climates of learning. Too often the best-case scenario is that cultural diversity is absent or invisible; the worst-case scenario is that it is actively resisted and denied. Feelings of isolation, alienation, anger, and helplessness result. Schools do not present caring and supportive climates conducive to maximum learning for all students when their programs and personnel ignore, distort, or demean culturally pluralistic identities, cultures, or experiences. As students' sense of selfhood is diminished, there is a corresponding decline in feelings of competence and in the frequency and quality of participation in the instructional process.

In addition, students may experience stress and anxiety in the routine operations of classrooms because the expectations and climate are very different from those of their cultural communities. These mismatches create feelings of uncertainty, insignificance, frustration, and incompetence, which in turn can lead to tensions and animosities between students and teachers. The effort and energy consumed by resolving these conflicts compete with attention needed for academic tasks. Mental energies that might be devoted to learning tasks are diverted to solving these psychological and emotional dilemmas. Consequently, engaged time on academic tasks, attention span, level of intellectual effort, and subsequent academic achievement suffer. Students in this situation ponder: "If I act ethnic, I am going to get into trouble with teachers, but if I don't, the other kids from my ethnic group will think I am a sell-out. What am I to do?" "Why should I try to learn what teachers want me to when they don't care anything about me?" "Just because Latino or Vietnamese students hang out together, teachers think they are gang wannabes and are trying to start trouble, but they don't say anything to White kids who do the same thing. Why are they always picking on us?" Or, "Why does the teacher think I should know about a bunch of old Latinos just because I have a Spanish name? Doesn't she realize how embarrassed I get when she starts talking about that stuff?"

Students with these kinds of feelings do not have a strong sense of security in their ethnic identity, and they are uncertain about how well they are accepted by teachers. They feel that they are being attacked psychologically, or perceive school as an alien and hostile environment. These dispositions mean that they are not able to concentrate as well as they might on academic tasks. Conversely, the sense of psychological well-being that results when students feel they are valued and cared about and that they belong leads to higher levels of personal confidence and competence, more learning efforts, and greater achievement outcomes. This is the rationale behind the multicultural idea that teaching culturally diverse content, perspectives, and experiences is essential to achieving a balanced and high-quality education for all students.

Whether the effect is positive or negative, teachers are "significant others" to students. Their attitudes toward cultural differences have a profound effect upon both majority and nonmajority students. Teachers' benign neglect of cultural diversity can lead some students to infer that it is of little or no importance. Others may take it as personal rejection, causing them to distrust teachers or reject all that teachers have to offer instructionally. For students who do not want to acknowledge and appreciate cultural diversity, teachers who avoid or denigrate it in the classroom are models of acceptable behavior to be emulated. Teachers cannot be supportive of the needs and potential of culturally diverse students without understanding their cultural values and expressive behaviors. They may misinterpret or fail to recognize a cry for help that is transmitted in cultural codes, and therefore ignore or mistreat it. For instance, some of what educators perceive as "gang wannabe behavior" among young teens may be nothing more than students trying to satisfy their psychological need to belong and to affiliate with their ethnic identity. Furthermore, schools' success in maximizing the learning of students from different ethnic, social, and racial backgrounds directly reflects the extent to which cultural pluralism is incorporated in all aspects of the educational process. This is especially true if there is any validity to the arguments that students who feel comfortable with who they are learn better, and that multicultural education improves self-concept and self-esteem for diverse learners.

Identity Development

General Principles:	Multicultural Translations:
• Self-acceptance leads to greater academic achievement.	• Ethnic identity development, self-concept, and academic achievement are interrelated.
• Improvement of individual abilities enhances personal competence of students.	• Ethnic identity is a major part of personal competence for diverse students.

Identity formation is another major psychological need of individuals that is paramount to general and multicultural principles of human development. It has many different dimensions. Among them are uniqueness, self-consistency, wholeness, continuity, competency, and psychosocial reciprocity (Conger and Petersen 1984). In other words, identity development is an interactive process involving individual and group, personal and social factors. For individuals to be confident and secure in themselves, there needs to be some consistency between how they see themselves and how significant others in their lives perceive them.

The point made earlier that educators are significant others to students is important here. Educators' influence on the identity and academic achievement of students is well established in research on teacher attitudes and expectations (Good and Brophy 1978). Students for whom teachers have high achievement expectations and personal acceptance tend to do much better in academic performance, as well as in social adjustment to school rules. Unfortunately, many teachers have negative attitudes toward, and low expectations for, students of color and of poverty. These can be accounted for, in part, by the fact that there is a growing social gap between students and teachers. Teachers in the United States are predominantly European-American, middle class, female, in their mid-40s, highly educated (having master's degrees or the equivalent), and living in suburbs or small communities bordering large cities. By comparison, the student population is increasingly composed of children of color, poor children, immigrants, speakers of languages other than English, and children who live in large urban areas (*Status of the American School Teacher* 1992; Stout 1993). The absence of shared living experiences and points of reference is a serious obstacle to successful teaching and learning. Complicating the situation further is the fact that teacher preparation programs still do not provide enough training in multicultural education and ethnic diversity to build strong cultural bridges between students and teachers. Thus, too many teachers arrive in classrooms with negative, biased, or confused attitudes about cultural diversity, and they have expectations of low performance for some groups and high anxiety and low confidence levels about teaching multicultural education. These factors generate instructional behaviors that have long-range effects on how African-American, Native American, Latino, Asian-American, and European-American students perceive themselves, their personal worth, and their academic competence—that is, their individual self-concepts, ethnic and cultural identities, and school achievement. Feelings of superiority among European-American students may be inadvertently reinforced; Japanese- and Chinese-American students may feel pressure to live up to the image of themselves as the "model minority" who are never disciplinary problems and always do well academically; and African-Americans may feel that academic failure is a foregone conclusion regardless of how hard they try to achieve.

To a large degree, educators' conceptions of personal identity as part of human development, and its place in the educational process, can be traced back to Erik Erikson (1968). He placed identity formation within the framework of eight major stages of personality development between infancy and adulthood. These are summarized in Figure 3.2.

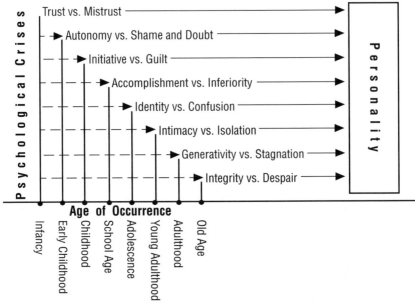

Figure 3.2 Erikson's Stages of Personality Development

Identity formation is placed within the framework of eight major stages of personality development between infancy and adulthood.

Source: Based on Erikson, E. H. 1968. *Identity, youth, and crisis.* New York: Norton.

Erikson suggested that "crisis" is endemic to the process of acquiring a mature and clarified identity, and such an identity is imperative for building a psychologically healthy adult personality. It is a crisis because the individual has to negotiate and resolve conflicts between shifting internal and external demands. The need to resolve conflicts between an integrated identity and role diffusion or confusion is present in all age groups, but it becomes a major issue during adolescence, when students are in middle school or high school. It is not until then that individuals have developed the prerequisite physical growth, mental maturation, and social responsibility needed to pass successfully through the crisis of identity. During early adolescence, the entire human organism goes through radical changes. It is hardly surprising, then, that identity development is among them, or that it has many different aspects or dimensions. Erikson concluded that the creation of a clarified identity is both simple and complex, universal and unique, positive and negative, normative and deviant, definitive and ambivalent, autonomous and dependent, coherent and certain, confusing and problematic. It is also affected by gender, race, class, ethnicity, nationality, microculture and macroculture, language, and community. A mature, clarified, and integrated identity is the foundation in which several other prized principles and goals of education are anchored. These include personal liberation, individual empowerment, social consciousness and competence, moral conviction and courage, improved academic achievement, and self-actualization.

Two of the components of identity development that are significant to adolescents are personal ego identity and sex-role identity. Publications on middle level education and early adolescent development offer myriad descriptions of how the behaviors and values of young adolescents are governed by their need to be accepted, peer pressures, perceived self-images, vacillations between independency and dependency, and often-exaggerated notions of gender attributes.

As people progress through different stages of ego and gender identity development, they become increasingly more competent in coping with life, solving personal and interpersonal problems, and accepting who they are. According to Conger and Petersen (1984, 82), those who achieve a strong clarified identity are:

> *likely to be more autonomous, less dependent on the views of others, more complex in their thinking, less constricted, more resistant to stress, and more creative. . . . They are also likely to show a greater capacity for intimacy with same- and opposite-sex peers, a more confident sexual identity, a more positive self-concept, a higher level of moral reasoning, and greater cultural sophistication. . . . In addition, they tend to be better liked by their peers, especially by those who have achieved a strong sense of identity themselves.*

Given these positive effects, it is understandable that teachers of both general education and multicultural education place heavy emphasis on helping students develop a positive self-concept, self-esteem, and self-image. It also explains why the theme, "Who am I," an obvious component of curriculum for the K–3 grades, is an issue of utmost importance in all schooling. While the earlier grades explore this question on a personal or *primordial* level, other grades examine it on a broader scale. Thus, when students are studying U.S. history, world cultures, and comparative literatures, the issue of identity as a member of a group, a nation, a culture, and the world is the common point of analysis.

Multiculturalists suggest that there is another component of identity that is equally as important as personal self-concept and gender. Erikson (1968) identified it in discussions of how his model operates when applied to African-Americans. This factor is ethnicity. As individuals from different ethnic groups and cultural backgrounds grapple with universal questions—"Who am I?" "How did I come to be?" and "What might I become?"—they cannot avoid reflecting on what it means to be African-American, European-American, Asian-American, Latino, or Native American. For students from these groups, fashioning a positive and clear ethnic identity is often complicated by the fact that society and schools frequently ignore or demean their ethnic groups and heritages. There is not a wide variety of easily accessible models—significant ethnic others—to use as yardsticks in constructing their own ethnic identity. Consequently, the journey toward ethnic self-acceptance can be frustrating, and even agonizing. Once schools and teachers accept ethnicity and culture as legitimate elements of psychological and educational development, adults can intervene appropriately to assist students through the process.

Boykin (1986) suggested that African-Americans experience a "triple quandary" in constructing their ethnic identity and achieving in school. They have to negotiate in three realms of experience simultaneously—the main-stream culture, their ethnic cultures, and the culture of membership in an oppressed and marginalized minority. Boykin's ideas apply to other ethnic groups of color as well. Individuals engaged in the resolution of these issues pass through developmental stages and sequences that approximate models of other types of identity formation (Erikson 1968; Marcia 1980) with similar results. These stages are assigned different labels, but the traits and effects are basically the same.

Each stage of ethnic identity development has its own distinguishing characteristics; there are also stylistic differences in making decisions, solving problems, processing information, and translating values into expressive behaviors. In other words, there is a strong correspondence between stages of ethnic identity and different ways of valuing, being, and behaving. Generally, the pattern of ethnic identity development begins with feelings of unaware- ness, denial, or disaffiliation. Individuals either are not conscious of what it means to be European-American, African-American, Japanese-American, or Puerto Rican, or they have distorted notions about these ethnic identities. These distortions may take the form of ethnocentrism ("My ethnic group is better than everyone else's"); assuming that everyone feels the same way about their ethnic group; feeling shame and embarrassment about member- ship in particular groups; and making deliberate efforts to deny one's ethnic identity.

From here, growth toward ethnic clarification and acceptance progresses through (1) a questioning stage where different bases for determining ethnic identity are sought, to (2) trying out new notions of ethnic identity, to (3) achieving genuine acceptance of ethnicity, based on a thorough under- standing of what it means personally, individually, socially, and collectively. As individuals advance through the stages they become increasingly competent in areas such as self-acceptance, academics, interpersonal relations, and social adaptations. These growth patterns have been described in detail by several researchers whose work focused primarily on groups of color, including Atkinson, Morten, and Sue (1979), Berzonsky and Sullivan (1992), Cross (1991), Gay (1985; 1987), Phinney (1989; 1992), and Streitmatter (1989). Helms (1990) and Tatum (1992) modified Cross's ethnic identity development model and applied it to European-American students. They found similar results with respect to how individuals' attitudes toward and interactions with other ethnic groups change as their own ethnic self-identity becomes increasingly clarified.

Thus, factors of race and ethnicity are as important to the formation of a clear and healthy identity as are individual personality traits and sexuality. Multicultural education is helpful both in understanding these factors and responding to them by designing instructional programs and practices. Self- concept, ethnic identity, and a sense of personal competence, all part of the identity development process, are too important in their own right, as well as in their effects on academic performance, to be ignored or left to happen- stance. This is why multicultural education contends that (1) achieving educa- tional equity and excellence is inextricably interrelated with culturally respon- sive teaching, and (2) understanding ethnicity and culture is essential to maximizing the human development of culturally different students.

Individuality and Universality

General Principles:	Multicultural Translations:
• Individual differences in human growth and development are normal.	• Ethnicity and culture are key determinants of individuality.
• Human dignity must be respected.	• Cultural socialization determines behavioral expressions of humanity.
• There are both similarities and differences among individuals and groups.	• Strengths and abilities are culturally contextual.
• Individual learning styles and preferences should be accommodated.	• Cultural filters diversify human potential.

Specialists in human development agree that the patterns of growth are the same for everyone, but that no individual experiences them in exactly the same way as another. This fact causes educators to emphasize the simultaneous uniqueness and universality of student growth and development. Similarities in developmental needs and differences in individual abilities give credence to the idea that education is a personal, as well as a group, process. In order to implement this, there must be *instructional variability within a unified framework of human growth and development.*

Gardner (1993) further explored these concepts in relation to intelligence. Intelligence, which he defined as "the ability to solve problems, or to create products, that are valued within one or more cultural settings" (Gardner 1993, x), is not monolithic, universal, or transcendent of cultural boundaries. Instead, like other dimensions of human development, it has multiple content, forms, and expressions that become meaningful *within situational and cultural contexts.* He identified seven "intelligences": linguistic, musical, logical-mathematical, spatial, bodily-kinesthetic, and intra- and interpersonal competencies. Each employs different means of acquiring or transmitting information, selecting materials to be mastered, determining ways of learning, and choosing the particular learning site of (Gardner 1993). Educational programs and instructional strategies must do likewise if they are to capitalize on the strengths of students, compensate for their weaknesses, expand their intellectual horizons, and help them maximize their human potential.

Intelligences should be perceived as interactions between certain individual proclivities on the one hand, and the opportunities and constraints that characterize particular settings on the other (Gardner 1993). Multicultural educators add that the criteria used to determine intelligence, and areas of intelligence dominance, are culturally determined as well. The importance that mainstream society attaches to linear, rational, and analytical thinking cultivates logical-mathematical intelligence. This focus fits well with the form—standardized tests—used most often to measure both intellectual potential and performance. Since African-American culture is anchored in relational logic and oral, musical, and performance traditions, it is not surprising that its members exhibit high levels of musical, bodily-kinesthetic, and interpersonal intelligences. Many authors, for example, Gay and Baber (1987); Heath (1989); King and Mitchell (1990); Kochman (1982); and Pasteur and Toldson (1982), have presented detailed and vivid descriptions of these. It should not be too surprising that these kinds of skills are not highly valued, transferable to school settings, or assessed by standardized tests, given the dominant value orientation of schools. Furthermore, how the abilities of some individuals are expressed behaviorally can differ markedly from those of others who have similar competencies but are from different ethnic and cultural backgrounds. A case in point is the test performance of European-American, Japanese-American, and Chinese-American students. On many of the measures of academic achievement, such as the National Assessment of Educational Progress (NAEP), these students have similar overall performance profiles. However, specific differences within these patterns exist. Japanese-American and Chinese-American students tend to perform better than European-American students on mathematics but not as well on verbal abilities (NCES 1993; Applebee, Langer, and Mills 1986).

Another indication that intelligence is contextual is the fact that competence in one setting does not necessarily transfer to other settings. Many examples are reported in ethnographic studies that describe the high levels of competence exhibited by African-American, Latino, and Native American students in various roles within their cultural communities, but not demonstrated in the school environment. One example is communicative and interpersonal skills among cultural and ethnic peers. Students who are very fluent and adept in expressing their ideas and thoughts outside of school cannot write a coherent paragraph in the classroom. Other graphic descriptions of this phenomenon have emerged from studies of Native Hawaiian and Native American students by Boggs, Watson-Gegeo, and McMillen (1985); Cazden, John, and Hymes (1985); and Trueba, Guthrie, and Au (1981). When the styles of learning in school were adjusted to be more similar to those used in their homes, students who were failing in school did a complete turnabout and performed very well on academic tasks. The *content* of their intelligence did not change at all; what changed were the *contextual* factors and frameworks provided for the students to demonstrate their intelligence.

It is imperative, then, to include *situation* and *context,* along with *multiplicity,* in educational plans designed to reflect and complement the intelligences of different students. Educators must recognize that the structures, forms, and procedures through which students are expected to demonstrate their abilities may obscure, rather than elucidate, intelligence. Stated somewhat differently, the problems that culturally different students have with achieving success in school may be more procedural than intellectual. They may have the knowledge, or the capability to learn, but may not know how to transmit it through the methods used in schools. This phenomenon is analogous to the degree of understanding and the level of production in second language learning. Many English speakers learning French as a second language may be able to read and understand more than is evident in their French *listening and speaking* capabilities. And just because limited English proficiency (LEP) or dialect speakers have not mastered the form of standard English communication does not mean that they are not intelligent. These "situational competences" underscore the need for teachers to use many different instructional techniques that are culturally sensitive to tap the various intellectual abilities of students.

Understanding the concept of situational competence should prevent educators from assuming that just because culturally different students do not demonstrate intelligence according to school standards, they are not intelligent. It should also lead to a greater appreciation of the ways different cultures characterize, celebrate, and award intelligence. More will be said about this in Chapter 5, where learning and teaching styles are discussed.

Conventional educational thought contends that schooling must celebrate personal uniqueness but treat all students the same. This is possible because every person is a human being but is unique in specific development, mental abilities, social and emotional behavior, and total personality. As Lefrancois (1988, 122) explained:

> *We are not products of a single blueprint, put through the same assembly line, and appearing, identical and fully formed, ready to learn, on the educational scene. Rather, each of us is a unique model—a function of different genetic recipes and different environmental forces.*

At the same time, all of us are, in some ways, like everyone else. We share certain elements of the human blueprint of attributions, growth, and developmental traits. This is why so many teachers resist suggestions that ethnic and cultural differences should be discussed openly in classrooms. Yet, real individual and group differences are apparent in all levels of life and living. All students have intellectual ability, but the level and kind differ. Everyone learns to speak a language, but obviously not always English, let alone the same dialect of English. All children have families, but what constitutes a family differs by ethnic, social, and cultural group. All groups have standards of acceptable and unacceptable behavior in social interactions, but the specific ways in which these are enforced through sanctions and celebrations vary greatly. All groups have criteria for success, but the *content* of success is culturally determined. Given these differences and similarities, it is virtually impossible that any claim schools make about facilitating the human and individual development of students can be valid if they do not give serious attention to how culture shapes individuality and universal humanity.

Multicultural educators agree that developing both individual and universal humanity of students is necessary, but they feel that these qualities cannot be separated from culture. Human beings develop personality and character through socialization processes that are always framed within specific cultural, ethnic, and social contexts. Everyone belongs to cultural and ethnic groups, although the types and intensity of membership may vary widely. These cultural and ethnic affiliations are necessary for healthy survival (García 1982). This position is congruent with Dewey's (1897; 1902) suggestions that individuals are biological, psychological, and sociological beings, and that none of these dimensions of human potential should be compromised or subordinated to the others. Similarly, the educational process should have a biological, psychological, and sociological side. "The child's own instincts and powers furnish the material and give the starting point for all education. . . . but we do not know what these mean until we can translate them into their social equivalents" (Dewey 1897, 4–5).

Multicultural education is an important set of instructional techniques for translating the "raw material" of individual intellectual potential into "social equivalents" for students from different ethnic groups and cultural backgrounds. It uses "culture" and "biology" as bases for justifying its emphasis on using different strategies to develop common human qualities. Embedded in this emphasis is the notion that individual values, attitudes, and potentials are expressed in actual behaviors that vary widely because they are shaped by an interaction of biological inheritance, social experiences, and cultural conditioning. Culture is a critical screen for educators to use in understanding all dimensions of human development and understanding what they imply for designing and implementing educational programs. For example, the cultural backgrounds of Native American students, which give priority to the group over the individual, may inhibit the initiative and competitiveness that educators cultivate and reward in schools. Their culture's conceptions of time and harmony with nature may lead to a pace in performing tasks that teachers view as "reluctance" or "nonengagement." Teachers, using their own cultural lenses to interpret the behavior, might believe that students are not motivated, or that they don't take responsibility for their own learning.

While this tendency to generalize one's own values and methods to others is understandable, in culturally diverse classrooms it can be devastating to the success of teaching and learning. It ignores the fact that people are much more than mere biological organisms or even unique individuals; they are cultural beings and members of groups (Kallen 1970). Before them in time, within them in quality, and surrounding them in influence are their ancestors, relatives, and kin. It is within this historical, interpersonal, and cultural context that students live, value, and acquire identity. It is also where and how they come closer to capitalizing on their personal strengths and maximizing their human potential. Without a cultural framework to provide applied meaning to raw, undifferentiated potential, individuality and humanity are mere theoretical abstractions, if not complete illusions. Therefore, teachers need to understand how biological, sociological, hereditary, and environmental factors combine to shape the uniqueness and humanity of every individual student, and how instructional programs should reflect these understandings.

A companion explanation to culture, for using diversity in curriculum and instruction, is biological inheritance. Multiculturalists remind us that no two humans are biologically identical, just as no two individuals are culturally and socially identical. This is a hallmark feature of humans. Therefore, treating students the same while recognizing individual differences is literally and practically impossible on all counts. Philosophically and conceptually, these two ideas are not reconcilable when the standard of sameness is the diversity and uniqueness of everyone. The only way to ensure that everyone is treated the same is to treat everyone differently! The degree to which diversity of all kinds pervades practice is a measure of how close the educational process comes to genuinely recognizing the uniqueness of individuals and the universality of their humanity.

Multicultural education facilitates this process by introducing dimensions of individuality and humanity that are nested in ethnicity, race, social class, culture, language, historical experiences, and national origins. Heretofore, these factors have not been adequately considered in educational decision making. Yet, they increase the validity, relevance, and effectiveness of the educational process for all students, including those from oppressed ethnic and cultural groups in the United States as well as those from European-American, middle-class, mainstream groups who are victimized by false notions about the superiority and universality of their culture.

Reflections and Applications

The undeniable fact of life is that people are different. This is an inherent part of their human inheritance. The sources of these differences vary widely, as do their manifestations in attitudes, values, behaviors, and learning potentials. Factors central to this variability are biological heredity, cultural socialization, contextual settings, and developmental rates, but these differences are not necessarily disadvantages or limitations that restrict or minimize learning. They are positive attributes that can be used to translate general principles into practical possibilities of specific groups and to serve as benchmarks of the quality of educational programs and experiences for all students.

Both general education and multicultural education agree on certain basic principles of human development:

1. Development is holistic and universal, but not uniform; that is, all parts (physical, mental, social, moral) of the human organism are engaged at the same time but progress does not occur at the same rate;
2. Development follows a continuous, orderly, and progressive sequence; and
3. As the developmental process advances, individuals become increasingly more independent, confident, capable, and complex in academic, personal, and social skills.

Whereas general education theory approaches human developmental factors at high levels of conceptual and generalized abstraction, multicultural education interprets them operationally and with greater contextual specificity. These patterns of growth have important implications for providing quality educational programs and practices for students in a culturally pluralistic society. To make educational experiences developmentally appropriate and maximally relevant for U.S. students, they need to be culturally pluralistic and sensitive to the diversity of needs, skills, interests, and growth rates inherent in the human condition.

These realizations are part of the underlying reasoning for the priority that general education gives to teaching the whole child by matching curriculum and instruction to the developmental readiness levels of students and by using instructional strategies that have multiple sensory appeal and a variety of learning outcome potentials. In multicultural education, these ideas form the foundation for using alternative instructional means to achieve common learning outcomes, placing general principles of pedagogy into the framework of cultural diversity, and matching teaching techniques with culturally different learning styles. All of these ideas offer promising possibilities for translating the principles of child-centered, developmentally appropriate, and relevant education into a variety of classroom practices for children who differ in many ways—biologically, psychologically, socially, and culturally.

The different perceptions and principles of human growth and development presented in this chapter have many implications for teaching and learning. Some of these were stated explicitly and others indirectly. Now is the time for you to think about other practical applications. The following activities offer some possibilities and may generate others.

1. Review the "Inventory of Personal Development Techniques" that you began to develop at the beginning of this chapter (page 65). In view of the insights you have gained from reading this chapter, revise, refine, or even replace your inventory and make it more culturally sensitive.

2. Consult a developmental or educational psychology textbook to identify general characteristics attributed to different age groups, such as young childhood (3–5 years old), middle childhood (6–9 years old), early adolescence (10–14 years old), late adolescence, and young adulthood. Select for study one age group appropriate to your teaching assignment. Analyze the list of traits to determine how much or how little of it is sensitive to cultural differences in developmental patterns. Choose a specific ethnic or cultural group in your school, such as European-, African-, Filipino-, Appalachian-, Hmong-, or Mexican-American, on which to focus. Observe students from this group for a given period of time (one or two weeks) to see if or how they manifest the characteristics attributed to their age group. Based on what you see, either (a) revise the list of characteristics to reflect your observations or (b) currently contextualize the traits by providing a behavioral example of how they are expressed or demonstrated by the students you observed.

3. Ask students in your class to develop an "I am _____" portrait of themselves by using descriptive adjectives such as "I am imaginative, inspiring, curious, energetic." Then have them create a visual image of their self-portrait, such as a photo essay, collage, videotape presentation, or painting. Compare the portraitures to see if there are any discernible differences by ethnicity or gender.

4. Assess how your school transmits messages about the development of individuality and the humanity of students through its institutional

"symbols and signs." Examine such things as the school's motto, song, decorations, rules of decorum, award ceremonies, and disciplinary policies. What kinds of values are embedded in these "symbols and signs"? To what extent do they reflect cultural diversity? How can these signs and symbols be changed or extended to convey the idea that different types of ethnicity and elements of cultural socialization are valued contributors to individual and human development? If you teach in the fourth grade or above, you could have your students participate in this activity as well.

5. Read further about ethnic identity development in order to identify and describe the different stages of the process, for example, Gay (1985), Phinney (1989), and Tatum (1992). Use the stage descriptors to create an observation scale. Choose two ethnic groups in your school to observe, and see how they exhibit the ethnic identity stages. Then, (a) list some descriptive behaviors for each stage as expressed by the students from each of the ethnic groups you chose to observe; (b) compare the two groups to determine stage dominance, and differences and similarities in types of behaviors within stages; and (c) think about some ways your school's programs and procedures can be modified to be more responsive to the general characteristics of each stage of ethnic identity, and the specific behavioral expressions of the students you observed.

References

Applebee, A. N., J. A. Langer, and I. V. S. Mills. 1986. *The writing report card: Writing achievement in American schools.* Princeton, N.J.: Educational Testing Service.

Atkinson, D. R., G. Morten, and D. W. Sue. 1979. Proposed minority identity development model. In *Counseling American minorities: A cross-cultural perspective,* ed. D. R. Atkinson, G. Morten, and D. W. Sue, 191–200. Dubuque, Iowa: William C. Brown.

Berzonsky, M. D., and C. Sullivan. 1992. Social-cognitive aspects of identity style: Need for cognition, experiential openness, and introspection. *Journal of Adolescent Research* 7: 140–55.

Boggs, S. T., K. Watson-Gegeo, and G. McMillen. 1985. *Speaking, relating, and learning: A study of Hawaiian children at home and at school.* Norwood, N.J.: Ablex.

Boykin, W. 1986. The triple quandary and the schooling of Afro-American children. In *The school achievement of minority children: New perspectives*, ed. U. Neisser, 57–91. Hillsdale, N.J.: Lawrence Erlbaum.

Cazden, C. B., V. P. John, and D. Hymes., eds. 1985. *Functions of language in the classroom*. New York: Teachers College.

Combs, A. W., and D. Snygg. 1959. *Individual behavior: A perceptual approach to behavior*. New York: Harper and Row.

Conger, J. J., and A. C. Petersen. 1984. *Adolescence and youth: Psychological development in a changing world*. New York: Harper and Row.

Cross, W. E., Jr. 1991. *Shades of black: Diversity in African American identity*. Philadelphia: Temple University Press.

Dewey, J. 1897. *My pedagogic creed*. New York: Macmillan.

Dewey, J. 1902. *The child and the curriculum*. Chicago: The University of Chicago Press.

Erikson, E. H. 1968. *Identity: Youth and crisis*. New York: Norton.

Fordham, S., and J. U. Ogbu. 1986. Black students' school success: Coping with the "burden of 'acting white'." *The Urban Review* 18(1): 76–206.

García, R. L. 1982. *Teaching in a pluralistic society: Concepts, models, strategies*. New York: Harper and Row.

Gardner, H. 1993. *Frames of mind: The theory of multiple intelligences*. New York: Basic Books.

Gay, G. 1985. Implications of selected models of ethnic identity development for educators. *Journal of Negro Education* 54: 43–55.

Gay, G. 1987. Ethnic identity development and black expressiveness. In *Expressively black: The cultural basis of ethnic identity*, ed. G. Gay and W. L. Baber, 35–74. New York: Praeger.

Gay, G., and W. L. Baber. 1987. *Expressively black: The cultural basis of ethnic identity*. New York: Praeger.

Good, G. L., and J. E. Brophy. 1978. *Looking in classrooms*. New York: Harper and Row.

Heath, S.B. 1989. Oral and literate traditions among black Americans living in poverty. *American Psychologist* 44: 367–73.

Hedges, W. D., and M. L. Martinello. 1977. What the schools might do: Some alternatives for the here and now. In *Feeling, valuing, and the art of growing: Insights into the affective*, ed. L. M. Berman and J. A. Roderick, 229–47. Washington, D.C.: ASCD.

Helms, J. E., ed. 1990. *Black and white racial identity: Theory, research, and practice*. Westport, Conn.: Greenwood Press.

Holliday, B. 1985. Towards a model of teacher-child transactional processes affecting black children's academic achievement. *In Beginnings: The social and affective development of black children*, ed. M.B. Spencer, G.K. Brookins, and W.R. Allen, 117–30. Hillsdale, N.J.: Lawrence Erlbaum.

Kallen, H. M. 1970. *Culture and democracy in the United States.* New York: Arno Press and the *New York Times.*

King, J., and C. Mitchell. 1990. Black mothers to sons: Juxtaposing African American literature with social practice. New York: Peter Lang Publishers.

Kochman, T. 1982. *Black and white styles in conflict.* Chicago: The University of Chicago Press.

Lefrancois, G. R. 1988. *Psychology of teaching.* Belmont, Calif.: Wadsworth.

Loree, M. R. 1970. *Psychology of education.* New York: The Ronald Press.

Marcia, J. 1980. Identity in adolescence. In *Handbook on adolescent psychology,* ed. J. Adelson, 159–87. New York: Wiley.

Maslow, A. H. 1954. *Motivation and personality.* New York: Harper and Row.

National Center for Education Statistics (NCES). 1993. *The condition of education.* Washington, D.C.: U.S. Department of Education, Office of Educational Research and Information.

National Education Association (NEA). *Status of the American school teacher, 1990–91.* 1992. Washington, D.C.: NEA.

Ogbu, J. U. 1992. Understanding cultural diversity and learning. *Educational Researcher* 21(8): 5–14, 24.

Pasteur, A. B., and I. L. Toldson. 1982. *Roots of soul: The psychology of black expressiveness.* Garden City, N.Y.: Anchor Press.

Phinney, J. S. 1989. Stages of ethnic identity development in minority group adolescents. *Journal of Early Adolescence* 9: 34–49.

Phinney, J. S. 1992. The multigroup ethnic identity measure: A new scale for use with diverse groups. *Journal of Adolescent Research* 7: 156–76.

Roderick, J. A. 1977. Describing persons in settings: Making the affect explicit. In *Feeling, valuing, and the art of growing: Insights into the affective,* ed. L. M. Berman and J. A. Roderick, 203–27. Washington, D.C.: ASCD.

Simpson, E. L. 1977. The person in community: The need to belong. In *Feeling, valuing, and the art of growing: Insights into the affective,* ed. L. M. Berman and J. A. Roderick, 181–98. Washington, D.C.: ASCD.

Stout, R. T. 1993. Enhancement of public education excellence. *Education and Urban Society* 25(3): 300–10.

Streitmatter, J. L. 1989. Identity development and academic achievement in early adolescence. *Journal of Early Adolescence* 9: 99–116.

Tatum, B. D. 1992. Talking about race, learning about racism: The application of racial identity development theory in the classroom. *Harvard Educational Review* 62(1): 1–24.

Trueba, H. T., G. P. Guthrie, and K. H. P. Au , eds. 1981. *Culture and the bilingual classroom: Studies in classroom ethnography.* Rowley, Mass.: Newbury House.

Chapter 4

Principles for Democratic Citizenship

Democracy and excellence are compatible. Education is their broker. Democracy is the rule of citizens, and citizens alone are free. For citizens are self-conscious, critical participants in communities of common speech, common value, and common work that bridge both space and time. As freedom yields community, so the forms of community and commonality alone yield freedom. Education makes citizens; only citizens can forge freedom. Democracy allows people to govern themselves; indeed, it insists that they do so. Education teaches them the liberty that makes self-government possible.

(Barber 1992, 265)

Education is supposed to serve the population for whom it is designed and the society in which it exists. In the United States, this means the educational process should be *democratic* in structure, purpose, content, and character. The same principles and ideals attributed to our political system of democracy apply to education as well. Just as the government is considered to be of, by, and for the people, education should have similar characteristics and intentions: to embody the heritages and legacies of the people; to be determined and controlled by the people; and to serve the needs and interests of the people. The operative question binding general education and multicultural education equally to these concepts is, Who are the people?

If you are not already familiar with them, find out the ethnic, gender, age, and social class profiles of our country's general and school populations. A good source for this information is the *Statistical Abstract of the United States,* published yearly by the Bureau of the Census. Another source is *The Condition of Education,* an annual publication by the United States Department of Education, Office of Educational Research and Improvement. Compare these figures to those for your own local schools and community.

The social service goals of education are designed to prepare students for their citizenship roles and responsibilities in society. They are shaped by a set of dual-focused functions that include adaptation and innovation; affirmation and reformation; continuity and change; transmission and transformation;

promoting ideals and understanding realities; teaching the special one and the common many. These purposes establish close and reciprocal relationships between personal and social development, individuals and groups, and principles of general and multicultural education. Roughly speaking, principles of general education for citizenship provide the valuative *contextual framework* for citizenship education, while multicultural education offers specific *textual references* for their application. Schools evoke the democratic values of the country when they promise a free, equal, and excellent education for all students. Multicultural education applies these values specifically to culturally different students by establishing conditions of excellence and equity for educational materials, experiences, and outcomes for Latino, Native American, Asian-American, African-American, and European-American students, as well as for our society. The ultimate ideal of both general and multicultural education is to create an educational foundation for an open, equal, moral, and just society for everyone. However, suggestions of how this ideal should be operationalized differ both within and among various groups of general and multicultural educators.

This chapter is organized into two major parts. The first provides a conceptual framework for understanding the source and focus of principles of education for citizenship and socialization. The second deals with the specific principles of citizenship education listed in Table 1.2 in Chapter 1 (see page 22). This discussion is organized according to three major themes represented by these principles: *the right to an education, conscience and community,* and *representation and participation.* The discussion of each theme begins with shortened versions of the principles from Table 1.2 and their multicultural translations. These are followed by a detailed analysis.

Conceptual Contours

Observations made by John Dewey almost 100 years ago in *My Pedagogic Creed* (1897) capture the flavor and significance of the social and civic value commitments or principles of U.S. education. Dewey extended these 20 years later in *Democracy and Education* (1916). Another influential and informative classic reference on the basic principles of U.S. education is Philip Phenix's *Education and the Common Good,* published in 1961. Although these books were written many years ago, the ideas they present are still relevant today. They are both *timely* and *timeless*—of particular relevance to the specific time and context in which they are initiated, as well as transcendent of any given temporal or environmental context, and therefore apropos to all. For these reasons, Dewey and Phenix are referenced frequently in establishing the parameters of principles of education for democratic citizenship.

Two themes in Dewey's and Phenix's works comprise the heart of educational principles for citizenship: *sociality* and *democracy*. According to Dewey, individuals are social beings with a natural need for community, and society is an organic union of these individuals. But, society and community are not achieved merely by having people live in close physical proximity to each other; rather, they result from the existence of common purposes and a commitment to act collaboratively to accomplish them. None of this is possible without some compromise between different interests, groups, and individuals. Similar ideas are espoused by proponents of cultural pluralism and multicultural education. They suggest that simply because many different groups live in the United States, this does not mean that they are strongly connected to each other or that feelings of affiliation among them will develop automatically. Creating a cohesive society out of this country's incredible diversity requires knowledge, skills, and values that can, and should, be taught.

The process and product of education for democracy should always have a social and experiential dimension. Dewey (1916, 7) explained:

> Not only does social life demand teaching and learning
> for its own permanence, but the very process of living
> together educates. It enlarges and enlightens experience; it
> stimulates and enriches imagination; it creates responsi-
> bility for accuracy and vividness of statement and thought.

Furthermore, education acts as an agency for the formation of individual character traits that are compatible with societal norms; transmits the cumulative knowledge and values of civilization; develops social consciousness; and is the ultimate means of continuous social progress and reconstruction. However, education's social processes and functions have no definite meaning until the contexts in which they operate are identified and the kind of society we desire is defined. Thus, the knowledge base of a pluralistic society that recognizes that all segments of its population make worthy contributions is very different from one that is monocultural.

To say that education is a social function is to acknowledge from the outset some of its major distinguishing traits. First, its specific details will vary according to the nature of the context and the quality of life of the groups for which it is intended (Dewey 1916). Second, education is not a neutral or objective enterprise in content, form, or function. All of its dimensions are influenced by certain cultural values and convictions about what is important to know and to become, and why.

The priority we give to individual effort and competition in learning reflects the cultural values of the rugged individualism, the work ethic, and the autonomy of mainstream society. Cagan (1978, 229) presented a powerful explanation of this point:

> *Perhaps no other aspect of American social thought and culture is as widely acknowledged and deeply felt as that of individualism. The moral and political primacy of the individual over the group is often presented as the corner-stone of democratic society. Personal liberty, individual initiative, and the private search for happiness are values and ideas deeply rooted in the fabric of American society; if they do not accurately reflect the realities of life in this country, they do represent its ideal description. Americans have always valued the freedom to pursue their own inter-ests and the ability to attain personal goals through their own efforts, even when these are more apparent than real.*

It is not surprising that people who worked hard to attain an industrial and technologically advanced society place a high value on work, punctuality, and orderliness; nor is it surprising that these values would become a major part of the education that schools transmit to youth as part of their socializa-tion for U.S. citizenship (Taba 1962). The problem lies in assuming that these values and standards are "the best there is" and are universally correct for everyone. Teaching social values is a fundamental obligation and action of education. The challenge for schools is teaching values that include the viewpoints and experiences of the full range of ethnic and cultural groups that comprise the United States.

For Phenix (1961) the most important educational values for democratic living were the pursuit of goodness and truth, and excellence in being and doing for both individuals and society. Within this framework, democracy is more of a standard of living and a moral imperative for behavior than it is simply a political system. Phenix (1961) noted that it refers to all aspects of life, the establishment of universal principles of conduct, and the belief that everyone is worthy. Democracy is equitable and promotes just behaviors that insure that no individuals or groups will arbitrarily and capriciously exercise power and control over others. It represents rule by the laws of ethics and morality. It also incorporates a devotion to freedom, equality, and excellence in all human endeavors. The pivotal values of excellence to be developed in a democracy are intelligence, conscience, creativity, and community.

Dewey (1916, 101) added that democracy is "primarily a mode of associated living, of conjoint communicated experience." Its hallmark traits are the existence of shared common needs and interests, diversity of motivation and variation in responsive behaviors, mutually supportive relationships, and continuing changes in social habits to promote the common good.

Banks's (1993) and Sleeter and Grant's (1988) descriptions of multicultural education are similar to Phenix's and Dewey's descriptions of democracy. Banks (1993) viewed multicultural education as a concept, movement, and process designed to deliver equal educational opportunities to all students. It is a visionary goal by which school practice can be directed, guided, and evaluated. Sleeter and Grant (1988, 175) perceived multicultural education as "a different orientation toward the whole education process."

These values form the American creed as embodied in such preeminent documents as the Declaration of Independence, the Preamble to the Constitution, and Abraham Lincoln's Gettysburg Address. They are universal ethical guidelines for living together in society. Their universality derives from their relevance and appeal to all humans and from their potential to elicit every person's loyalty (Phenix 1961). In practice, however, these values appear in a wide variety of forms, actions, and expressions. What is good, true, right, just, and excellent is determined within particular situations and contexts, rather than in cosmic abstractions. Herein lies a critical connection between general education and multicultural education.

Education as a Basic Right

General Principles:	Multicultural Translations:
• Everyone has a right to a free and public education.	• The public is culturally pluralistic.
• Education serves society.	• To serve society, education must be culturally pluralistic.

Both multicultural and general education believe that a free and public education is a right of citizenship and a condition of democracy in the United States. As a public enterprise, it is both for and about the masses of the people, not simply the privileged few. This means that everyone—the common folk as well as advantaged individuals—should have equal access to the benefits of education, an unrestricted right to participate and be represented in its policies and programs, and shared responsibility for its support. As a right, education should be relevant to and of high quality for all citizens and all facets of society. It should be realistic, functional, enriching, and enabling. Good education for citizens and societies helps them to be their best in the present and to strive toward an even better future. Since culturally different individuals fall into all categories—citizens, public, common folk, and advantaged individuals—education must also be culturally pluralistic. Otherwise, a fundamental right of citizenship is systematically violated.

Educators who are not committed to cultural diversity tend to use the concept of majority rule to determine who the public is and to set the standards for selecting content and skills to be taught to students. They contend that since the majority of people in the United States have European origins, it is natural for their cultures and values to establish the normative standards of the national culture and all of its subsidiary institutions, including schools. When people decide to live in a given society, they enter into a tacit social contract to live by the rules and regulations of that society. In the United States, a key provision of this contract is that, while minority rights will be respected and can be practiced largely unencumbered in private, majority rule will prevail in public life. The purpose of education is to help enforce this social contract and perpetuate the national culture by socializing all individuals into its common features. In this way, it serves as a national unifier, liberator, equalizer, and common denominator for all the diverse strands of people and experiences that comprise the nation (Butts 1978). Essentially, this is the position teachers are taking when they proclaim, "In school all students need to learn how to act and talk properly if they expect to get a job and function in society. Culturally different students can practice their native languages and lifestyles in private, but in the public arenas, English and mainstream culture should prevail."

Multicultural educators do not reject the idea that the majority should rule, but they do question some commonly held notions. One is the extent to which the First Amendment provisions of the Constitution are honored in practice. These passages were added to the Constitution to protect minority religions, opinions, and beliefs, and to prevent the majority from becoming oppressive, dictatorial, and capricious in the exercise of its rights. Thus, if majority decisions in society are racist, then they are wrong, and the groups negatively affected by these actions have the right to seek redress. However, the historical record of the United States shows that many people who have not been targets of oppression and discrimination themselves have sympathized with oppressed groups and joined ranks with them in their struggles for freedom, equality, and justice. The opposition to slavery and the 1960s Civil Rights Movement are graphic examples of these trends.

The existence of "coalitions among freedom fighters" prompts a challenge to another common interpretation of majority rule—that "majority" is always a numerical concept. Multicultural educators contend that, when applied to issues of culture and community in pluralistic settings, majority rule is more a matter of "plurality of influence" than numbers. All ethnic, racial, social, and cultural groups in the United States have been, and are, instrumental in shaping its history, life, and culture. The result is a national majority culture that is more a synergy of pluralistic contributions than the domination of European-Americans, even though the contributions and full participation of all ethnic groups have not been acknowledged. Cruse (1987) suggested that the intent of the school desegregation and broader civil rights movements of the 1960s was to make society recognize, reflect, and accommodate the culturally pluralistic composition of all of its component parts. In other words, the ideal was for society to be "plural but equal." Because the people and the culture of the United States are a conglomeration of racially, ethnically, culturally, and socially diverse individuals, groups, and influences, this is the true "majority" that should govern.

Education in the United States is a public creation, a public mandate, and a public service. Undeniably, the "American Public" is becoming increasingly pluralistic. We saw evidence of this in Chapter 1. To serve its constituency adequately, education must likewise be culturally pluralistic. In symbol and substance it should convey to all students that they and their heritages are important components of what constitutes the essence of society's cultures, values, and ideals. That is, individuals from all social classes, and ethnic, racial, gender, language, and cultural groups have the right to be validated, to have unrestricted access to the full range of opportunities available to citizens, and to have a representative voice in decisions that affect their lives and destinies. The ethics and actions these values engender are necessary conditions for the support and survival of a democratic society. As Banks (1990, 211) explained, "To develop a clarified national identity and commitment to the nation, groups and individuals must feel that they are integral parts of the nation and national culture." Dewey (1916, 97–98) had earlier noted that:

> *all members of the group must have an equable opportunity to receive and to take from others. There must be a large variety of shared undertakings and experiences. Otherwise, the influences which educate some into masters, educate others into slaves. And the experience of each party loses in meaning when the free interchange of varying modes of life–experience is arrested.*

Another dimension of the right to education is access to knowledge that has value for personal affirmation and social utility. For the United States, this means learning about the cultures, experiences, and lifestyles of others, as well as being educated in one's own cultural traditions and styles. This is important because it is very unlikely that youth who are living and working today in monoracial or single-ethnic communities will live their adult lives in similar settings. Knowledge about cultural diversity will help students learn how to function better in a pluralistic society. Another reason for students to be sensitized to cultural diversity is the fact that it is already virtually impossible for any of us to live a day of our lives without being dependent on others. Consider, for example, where our food, clothing, transportation, communication technology, and recreation tools come from. They are both *multicultural* and *international*. We use automobile parts made in Germany, Korea, and Japan. Many of our clothes and shoes (or the raw materials for them) are made in Thailand, the Philippines, Korea, Italy, and Brazil. Within a given week, most of us are likely to eat several different kinds of ethnic foods or visit places where food is served by many ethnically diverse individuals. This global interdependence affects the quality of our daily lives. Students have the right to know who they are dependent upon for the convenience and richness of their everyday lives. They also need to examine critically how the policies and practices employed by the United States to meet its needs may lead to the exploitation or dislocation of peoples and cultures around the world.

For many students who are not fully assimilated into mainstream culture and society, such as African-Americans, Latinos, Asian-Americans, and Native Americans, the right to a culturally pluralistic education is reinforced by their dual or *bicultural identity*. These students have the right to maintain an identification with their cultures of origin while simultaneously learning and adopting mainstream cultural values and lifestyles. Rameriz and Castañeda (1974) and Darder (1991) referred to this as the right of all students to *cultural democracy*, which is a natural corollary to and extension of their right to *political democracy*. This means accepting the fact that the ways students communicate, relate, value, think, and learn are strongly influenced by their ethnic identity, background experiences, and value systems. To learn in educational environments—via instructional methods and from curriculum materials that are inclusive of their cultural orientations and reflect their group's contributions—is a birthright of citizenship and a pedagogical mandate for education in a culturally pluralistic society (Darder 1991; Rameriz and Castañeda 1974; Shade 1989).

Multiculturalists believe their approach to education can better prepare all students to live more productive, satisfying, and responsible lives in a society and world of increasingly diverse people, languages, and cultures. They are tools for translating the ideal of democratic rights into instructional programs for the maximal development of individual abilities and for helping students to understand their social responsibilities. Individualistic goals lead to personal competence and confidence that are prerequisites to social and civic involvement. The social responsibility need is met as students learn about the contributions of other groups, understand how the lives of groups and individuals are interrelated, and develop value commitments and action skills to work for the betterment of society for everyone's benefit. Together these learnings create a union of *pluribus* and *unum,* a pivotal concept in the democratic social experiment. Therefore, the civic, moral, cultural, and pedagogical implications of the right of all children to a high-quality education suggest that multicultural education is indeed the foundation and essence of all education for democratic citizenship.

Conscience and Community

General Principles:	Multicultural Translations:
• Community building is necessary for democracy.	• Community building requires knowing and valuing cultural diversity.
• Freedom, equality, and justice should be modeled by education.	• Freedom, equality, and justice are applied to culturally pluralistic issues and experiences.
• Interdependent relationships are understood.	• Cultural, ethnic, and social groups influence and are dependent on each other.
• National unity and a common culture are promoted.	• Cultural diversity, national unity, and a common culture are not contradictory.

Implicit in the right to an education was the idea that achievement of democratic values for all citizens requires a clear understanding that individual rights come with social responsibilities and that collective action is the best way to ensure both. Multicultural education and general education agree that democracy as a political and social system, as well as a philosophy of living, is a noble but imperfect experiment. They differ on what are the degrees of imperfection and where to place the emphasis and effort of future reform. Both recognize that, historically, the gains U.S. society has made toward achieving a true democracy have not been accomplished without struggle or multiethnic participation. This struggle has always involved questions of morality and cooperative group effort; issues of access and equality of opportunities; battles between the rights of the few and rights of the many; tensions between the individual and the community; needs to reconcile differences with similarities; quests for unity in the midst of plurality; and determination of who controls cultural truths (Barber 1992). Some powerful examples of struggles that illustrate how conscience and community come together in efforts to achieve democratic ideals are the Civil Rights Movement and the gender liberation movement.

Many contradictions and inconsistencies continue to exist between the ideal of democracy and its practiced realities. Alarming rates of racial and gender prejudices and inequities in educational, economic, and political opportunities permeate the entire fabric of society. Phenomenal progress is being made in medical science technology, extending longevity and improving the quality of life, yet incredibly high numbers of people die or are unhealthy because they cannot afford even basic medical care. The United States is a world leader in the production and consumption of goods and services, but many females and people from groups of color cannot earn enough money to live comfortable, secure, and dignified lives. Education has the obligation to prepare students to critically question inequities; to be morally outraged and intolerant of all forms of oppression, exploitation, and injustice; to understand the nature and effects of these problems—personally, nationally, and globally; to realize that their personal lives and the fate of society are inextricably interwoven; and to engage in constructive actions to eliminate all restrictions on individual rights and social possibilities. When ingrained, these attitudes, values, and skills create the kind of critical inquiry, civic responsibility, and communal interdependence that are essential to the preservation and extension of democracy.

Not only does true democracy require a foundation of shared values, experiences, and visions, but it depends upon shared moral convictions and ethical obligations as well. Freedom, equality, justice, and respect are the unrestricted prerogatives of every citizen of the United States, as long as they are not used to impose upon others or deny their rights. All children should be taught that they have the responsibility to claim and honor these prerogatives as their human and civic birthrights and to actively resist all actions that might compromise or constrain the same rights of anyone else. This knowledge is necessary for a genuine sense of community to evolve among diverse individuals, groups, interests, and concerns. Therefore, multicultural education recommends that all students learn how to recognize racism and its effects, how they are perpetuated, and how to engage in social and political actions to combat racism.

Students need to understand that people in society are so closely inter-connected that what happens to any one of them is significantly affected by what happens to everyone else. If some people in our society are oppressed and treated unfairly and if their human dignity is demeaned, then all people and all dimensions of society suffer. Freedom of speech and expression is indispensable for the maintenance and improvement of a democratic society. However, it cannot be used irresponsibly or capriciously to deny those with dissenting opinions the right to be heard. The concepts of interdependence and community operate in close conjunction with the democratic principles of freedom, equality, and justice. Macdonald (1977) even proposed that democracy is best represented not by concepts such as *liberty* or *equality* but by the commitment to *fraternity*. In his words, "It is concern for each as a brother-sister that provides the cornerstone of real democracy for a program built upon cultural pluralism" (Macdonald 1977, 13). Our nation's Poet Laureate, Maya Angelou (1993), delivered the same message in her reading of "On the Pulse of Morning" at President Bill Clinton's 1993 inauguration:

> *Here on the pulse of this new day*
> *You may have the grace to look up and out*
> *And into your sister's eyes,*
> *And into your brother's face,*
> *Your country,*
> *And say simply*
> *Very simply*
> *With hope—*
> *Good morning.*

These should be the anchor points of educational programs designed to teach skills for democratic citizenship because, as Kohn (1986, 67) explained, social change that benefits everyone can take place only "if collective action supersedes the quest for individual rewards." This is one of the most powerful strategy messages of multicultural education. It challenges the mainstream cultural competitive value of "I win, you lose," and replaces it with a coopera-tive one that says, in effect, "If we win, you win and I win."

John Dewey (1916) and Paulo Freire (1980), well-known proponents of education for democracy, offered additional strategies for achieving this goal. They suggested that schooling should be an apprenticeship for democratic living. Both believed that education should help students develop ethical foundations and moral convictions to guide their participation in the demo-cratic process and to develop a sense of communal obligation for the common good. Dewey (1916) proposed that students learn in environments and through activities where mutual interests and cooperative efforts are basic to achieving task mastery. Freire (1980, 28) added that democracy requires "dialogue, participation, political and social responsibility, as well as a degree of social and political solidarity."

Representation and Participation

General Principles:	Multicultural Translations:
• Everyone is enfranchised.	• Enfranchisement should be made available to oppressed and excluded groups.
• Citizens develop social competencies.	• Citizens should promote social change for ethnic, social, and cultural equality.
• Citizens develop knowledge and values consistent with democratic ideals.	• Citizens gain knowledge about diverse cultural groups from their own perspectives.
• Citizens promote intolerance of oppression.	• Citizens combat racism and cultural hegemony.

Multicultural interpretations of education for citizenship act as a critical voice, a civic conscience, and a reality filter for general education values and goals for democracy. They also offer some compelling perspectives on the need for all ethnic and cultural groups to be represented in educational programs and suggestions for accomplishing this. Four of these perspectives are presented here to illustrate how the principles of representation and participation operate when they are placed within a framework of cultural diversity.

First, multicultural education points out the incredible racial, cultural, ethnic, social class, linguistic, and national origin diversity that characterizes the informal and cultural aspects of U.S. society. However, formal operations, institutional structures, and power allocations are still dominated by Eurocentric, middle-class cultural values, individuals, and groups. The tension here is between a cultural democracy wherein all of this diversity is honored and a cultural hegemony that imposes the values, beliefs, and traditions of one group upon all others. Out of these cultural disparities emerges a very stratified, distorted, and often contradictory conception of who is "the public" or who are "the people" who comprise and control our society. Some segments of the public become more privileged or disadvantaged than others with respect to opportunities and outcomes, solely on the basis of their racial identity, gender, or social class. This violates the law, philosophy, and spirit of democracy.

A surface analysis gives the impression that the United States is more *culturally integrated* than it actually is. For instance, laws prohibiting racial segregation in education, housing, and employment mean that one can find people of different ethnic backgrounds in neighborhoods, businesses, and educational institutions. But this diversity is too often selective and peripheral. The rich social and cultural pluralism that exists in society has not penetrated the inner core of most institutions; nor does it necessarily impact, in any significant way, the personal lives of many individuals. Illustrations of this pattern are found in school administration and leadership, and middle- and upper-level corporate management. School principals and superintendents are predominantly European-American males, while classroom teachers continue to be mostly European-American females. Corporate managers are predominantly European-American males, but entry-level employees come from a wide variety of ethnic, cultural, and linguistic groups. Our experiences with desegregation have not yet touched the deeper levels of interpersonal relationships, since most people in the United States still live in relative isolation from people who differ from them racially, ethnically, and socially. In the most intimate and emotionally affirming dimensions of life, such as religion, residence, and primary interpersonal relationships, we tend to live in "ethnic enclaves," creating an image of many microcultures existing in close physical proximity to each other but not engaged in any significant, substantial, or quality interaction. Political activist Dick Gregory once observed, "The most segregated hour of the week is eleven o'clock on Sunday morning."

This segregation is still the norm both symbolically and literally, reflecting those parts of society that cultural pluralism has failed to penetrate. Many neighborhoods and schools claim to be "integrated" but the people who inhabit them do not spend quality time sharing experiences, issues, and concerns that make a *real* difference to them. These situations are both cause and effect of the growing gap between the "haves" and the "have nots," and the persistent resistance of many people to genuinely *embrace* cultural diversity. Consequently, cross-cultural, interracial, and socially diverse interactions continue to be infrequent, transitory, and perfunctory.

Education for democratic citizenship must build bridges across these boundaries if we expect ever to have a genuinely cohesive, caring, just, and egalitarian national community. These bridges must be varied, including geographic, interpersonal, communicative, cultural, and ethical ones. Once the "cultural bridges" are built, students need to be taught how to "cross the borderland" between cultures and to participate freely and fully in different cultural settings. Major steps toward achieving these goals include making certain that the contributions of different ethnic, cultural, and social groups are represented in school curricula and ensuring that these groups have access to all societal institutions.

A second multicultural perspective of principles of representation and participation presents many graphic reminders that morality cannot be legislated, and knowledge alone is not sufficient for social change. Although laws exist prohibiting discrimination and exclusion from participation in institutions on the basis of race, class, age, language, religion, or gender, society and schools continue to be plagued by disparities in opportunities. People who are considered highly intelligent by some standards may be morally corrupt and unethical in their social and interpersonal dealings with different ethnic individuals and groups. In the midst of declaring the sanctity of human dignity and the universality of human value, practices such as sexism, ageism, classism, and racism flourish, in opposition to these ideals. Economically, the United States is one of the wealthiest countries in the world, yet the number of children who are poor, hungry, homeless, or unhealthy increases daily. We say we believe in human dignity and high-quality living for everyone, but more equitable tax reforms and funding for social welfare services, health care, and education fail repeatedly to be endorsed and enacted into law. Many people still believe and behave according to the premises that (1) there is a single way to be "right," and those who do not ascribe to it are either inherently inferior, socially deviant, or in need of corrective intervention and paternalistic guidance, and (2) everyone can "make it" in U.S. society if they just try hard enough, and those who do not, lack initiative, motivation, and aspiration.

These situations are symbolic of gaps between ideals and realities, principles and practices, knowledge and morality, conscience and cognition, law and ethics, and of the need to combine these in the struggle to achieve a truly democratic society. They also illuminate Davidman and Davidman's (1994) description of multicultural education as "multifaceted." The changes it hopes to stimulate are so numerous and varied that they require multidimensional, interdisciplinary, and integrated approaches. Knowledge about cultural diversity has to be supplemented with values clarification to help students sort out their attitudes, beliefs, morality, and actions on issues related to freedom, equality, and justice within the context of a culturally pluralistic and ethnically diverse society. The contributions of culturally diverse groups and individuals must be included in the curriculum to correct for omission at the same time as changes occur in the fundamental structures and assumptions of the educational process. Students need to know how to make cultural diversity a more viable part of current society as they develop social and political skills to build an entirely new social order, far more egalitarian than the present one ever could be.

Phenix (1961) constructed a powerful argument in support of this kind of education agenda. He declared that all racist views and practices that restrict or limit the participation of some groups in schools and society are intolerable and undemocratic. Oppressive practices of all kinds should be counteracted through education that redistributes knowledge and power in order to challenge the privileged positions of the dominant group and its culturally hegemonic practices. The ultimate appeal should be to the principles of right, equality, dignity, and justice, which supersede intergroup rivalries. Thus, education for democratic citizenship in an ethnically and culturally pluralistic society should be devoted to breaking the bonds of racial hatred and exploitation and to promoting racial equality in their stead. Phenix (1961, 177) outlined key components of education for democratic citizenship:

The foundation of racial justice is a deep conviction of the unity of humanity and respect for the worth of every person. It is not enough to affirm these as abstract general principles; they must be controlling directives. Education for democratic race relations must go beyond factual instruction; it requires a change of motive, from that of promoting the prerogatives of one's own group to that of serving the right without calculation of personal advantage. This calls for a comprehensive reorientation, a total reversal of outlook which affects one's entire system of values.

Accomplishing this type of "reorientation" is a major purpose of multicultural education. Its successful completion will produce a stronger sense of affiliation and community among the different racial groups in the United States, as well as lead to psychological, social, political, intellectual, and aesthetic liberation of individuals. Consequently, education for racial justice is a critical component of both democratic citizenship and multicultural education within the United States.

Multicultural education underscores the fact that diversity is a definitive trait of humankind. Therefore, to be different is an inalienable right and deserves the kind of care and respect worthy of all things human. Schools and society in the United States, being merely small segments of humanity, should aspire to do no more and no less. The ultimate goal should be to have genuine pluralism present in all facets of education, without attaching any hierarchical order to its constituent parts. We come closer to achieving this goal when education includes an open analysis and thoughtful celebration of cultural diversity, combining knowledge acquisition with values clarification, moral and ethical commitments, and sociopolitical actions.

A third interpretation of the principles of participation and representation by multiculturalists suggests that education—if claiming to prepare students for citizenship in the United States and to make their rightful heritage accessible to them—must attend deliberately, forthrightly, conscientiously, and critically to cultural pluralism. The inescapable fact is that ethnic diversity and cultural pluralism are ever-present and determinant influences in U.S. history, life, and culture. Regardless of the subject educators use to transmit this legacy—

American history, American literature, American politics, American sociology, or American economics—the content and message are incomplete, if not totally false, when they do not include the contributions of different ethnic and cultural groups. Educators must also help students reconstruct what it means to be "American" and "human." In the process of redefinition, the perspectives, experiences, and contributions of all ethnic and cultural groups should be examined thoughtfully and thoroughly. Morrison (1992, 5–6) made this point eloquently, referring to the African-American influence shaping what is known as a unique "Americanness" in literature:

> *The contemplation of this black presence is central to any understanding of our national literature and should not be permitted to hover at the margins of literary imagination. . . . [I] wonder whether the major and championed characteristics of our national literature . . . are not in fact responses to a dark, abiding, signing Africanist presence. It has occurred to me that the very manner by which American literature distinguishes itself as a coherent entity exists because of this unsettled and unsettling population. . . . Through significant and underscored omissions, startling contradictions, heavily nuanced conflicts, through the way writers peopled their work with the signs and bodies of this presence—one can see that a real or fabricated Africanist presence was crucial to their sense of Americanness. And it shows.*

To proudly proclaim, "I am an American" (meaning a citizen of the United States), is to evoke a culturally pluralistic heritage. The idea of multiculturalism is new in name only. From the very beginning of its history, the United States's story has always been one of racial, geographic, religious, demographic, and cultural diversity in search of unity. The view of the United States as a nation of predominantly White European-Americans was never anything more than the hope and political imposition of a fraction of the immigrants to the United States and of the native peoples already here. Yet, we are not very comfortable with our diversity (Barber 1992). Multicultural educators believe this can be corrected by making all of our diversity visible, valued, and accessible to students, and by teaching them how to embrace it. This approach will lead to a stronger and more accurate sense of what it means to be American, a deeper respect for human dignity, and stronger feelings of community and camaraderie among diverse peoples. Individuals who understand how their lives are intertwined with those of others are less likely to engage in disrespectful, abusive, or oppressive actions. Thus, every individual and all aspects of society benefit from multicultural education, as it moves us closer to achieving social democracy and personal actualization.

A fourth perspective that multicultural education provides regarding the representative and participatory dimensions of education for democratic citizenship is that the cultural diversity that currently characterizes U.S. society has not reached its ultimate conclusion. The country is becoming daily more diverse. Ethnic demographics are literally changing the face of the United States (Henry 1990; Perry and Fraser 1993). Educational and sociological literature is inundated with growth statistics on ethnic and national origin groups and how these will be distributed in the nation's population during different time periods within the next century. The actual numbers may vary somewhat, depending upon the purposes and data sources of the projections, but the basic message is the same: the United States is becoming even more racially, ethnically, culturally, and linguistically diverse. Much of the cultural content of this diversity is fundamentally different from what the country is accustomed to, since the source of most of this growth is people of color who have come from parts of the world other than Western Europe. It adds dimensions and challenges to *e pluribus unum* that we have not even begun to recognize or understand. To be valid and realistic, the new normative standards in education and society will have to be cultural heterogeneity and plurality. Restructuring schools to reflect these changes is a reasonable expectation, since they are public institutions. As such, "they should be informed by the social realities of the communities they serve and representative of the vision of the society in which they exist" (Perry and Fraser 1993, 16).

While the principles of equality, freedom, justice, unity, and community are in no way compromised by the new ethnic demographics, the ways in which they are understood and practiced will have to change radically. One brief example illustrates this need. Consider the practice of using majority vote to approve policies and laws. As the population of the United States becomes more and more culturally and ethnically diverse in numbers and viewpoints, no single group will comprise a clear and definitive numerical majority. Increased knowledge and appreciation for cultural and ethnic diversity should mean that more people will engage in "cross-over politics" and vote on the merits of the issues rather than party and ethnic group lines. The two-party system of government may disappear entirely. In order to satisfy the social, political, economic, and educational demands of a very diverse population, more "rainbow" coalitions and more broadly based negotiated compromises will be required (Henry 1990). The United States also may need to modify its position as a monolingual society. The new standard for determining public policy on what language is used may have to be "plurality rule" instead of "majority rule," if cultural democracy rather than hegemony is to prevail. In some major cities and large school districts, such as Chicago, Los Angeles, New York, Milwaukee, and Miami, this new standard can already be observed.

Multicultural education advocates consider *plurality* and *diversity* to be the most viable frames of reference for translating into practice the right of all students to a relevant and excellent education, knowledge and skills for functioning in cross-cultural settings, and socialization for the citizenship that is nested in the culturally pluralistic realities that characterize the present and the future of U.S. society. A basic condition for achieving all of these goals is the representation and inclusion of cultural and ethnic diversity in all educational programs and practices. Some proponents refer to this inclusion process as "giving voice" to previously silenced or muted cultural groups and traditions by allowing them to "tell their own stories" (Darder 1991; Giroux 1992; McElroy-Johnson 1993). *Voice* is a validation process at the level of both principle and content. As principle, it is analogous to the democratic ideals of freedom of speech and the right to be actively involved in determining one's own destiny. As content, having voice means that the experiences and contributions of all cultural groups are included as worthwhile knowledge for students.

These demands are not unreasonable, given that few educators in the United States would take issue with the statement that schools are created by a society to teach students the knowledge, attitudes, values, and techniques that have cultural relevance, currency, and expediency (Taba 1962). Multicultural education meets all of these criteria. Furthermore, it incorporates principles of democracy; offers a teaching philosophy and methodology not tried before with culturally different students; and charts a course of action that has the potential to transform society.

Reflections and Applications

The ideas discussed in this chapter extend the meaning of principles of democracy and education for citizens by placing them within the context of cultural pluralism. From them emerges a clearer picture of why proponents of multicultural education declare that it is as American in origins, values, and intentions as general education. Both are grounded in the democratic ideals of freedom, equality, and justice, and view the primary task of schools as preparing youth for democratic citizenship and leadership. The fact that the United States is growing more and more culturally and ethnically diverse means that a permanent partnership is being forged between democracy and cultural pluralism. The democratic *text* can be understood practically only within a *context* of cultural pluralism. Democracy is impossible to achieve without the inclusion of cultural pluralism, and cultural pluralism rests on democratic values, ethics, and morality.

Therefore, the filters that multicultural education provides for making the abstract principles of freedom, equality, and justice more meaningful to the life experiences of culturally different groups are essential if genuine democracy is to be achieved. This makes multicultural education a necessity in education for citizenship, not a choice. This is what Banks(1991–92, 32) meant by declaring that multicultural education is "for freedom's sake."

Opportunities to practice increase the level of learning. Hopefully, you have learned many new things from reading this chapter. Your learning could be further enhanced by engaging in one or more of the activities and experiences suggested below.

1. Review your classroom routines to identify rules and regulations that you employ on a regular basis. These may be a list of "dos and don'ts," some general rules of social decorum, principles of behavior management and interpersonal interaction, or procedures for task performance. After you have completed your list, analyze it to see how many of the "democratic citizenship" values and principles discussed in this chapter are represented. A rule such as "Do not yell out answers; raise your hand and wait to be called on" might be interpreted as representing the principles of participation and equality of opportunity. Place the principles opposite the rules, and use these for a lesson on democratic citizenship rights, values, and responsibilities with your students.

2. Work with students and/or colleagues to create a "Bill of Rights for Cultural Diversity." Include information and insights gained from the discussion in this chapter. Your "Bill of Rights" can be generic, focusing on rights that apply in any school setting and subject. Or, it can be specific to a given subject area, such as English and language arts, science, mathematics, or humanities. After you have completed your list of rights, approach the entire faculty of your school to endorse and accept it as a statement of the value commitments of the school. Write your Bill of Rights in a form similar to the one that appears in the Constitution of the United States. Display it in a place of honor in the school and classroom. It then will become the "code of honor" for your school and classroom.

3. Schools transmit their commitment to democratic ideals and values in many different ways. Two of these are student handbooks and vision, philosophy, or mission statements. Schools frequently accept the mission or philosophy statement of the school district as their own. Examine the handbook and philosophy statement to see if you can extrapolate the particular democratic values that are embedded in the goals, statements, and rules and regulations. Then, suggest some ways these can be modified to include specifics about cultural diversity. For example, a student handbook rule that says, "All students will receive the same punishment for violating school rules," might be interpreted as an attempt to apply the democratic principle of "equality." A modification of this might include some culturally-specific extenuating circumstances when this rule would actually be unfair, such as students who do not know enough English to understand the rules.

4. Have your students work together cooperatively to develop an "Analytical Profile" of how the "right to an education" is distributed in practice throughout your school. Have them collect information such as who is enrolled in what kinds of classes (e.g., special education, advanced placement, vocational, "tough" vs. "easy," etc.) and extracurricular activities; who is elected to or selected for which leadership roles (e.g., honor society, student government, teaching assistant); who gets what kinds of awards and recognition; the percentage distribution of students, teachers, and administrators by ethnicity and gender; and how disciplinary actions are distributed by ethnicity, gender, and grade. After collecting the information, have the students compile it into comparative tables and charts, draw some interpretative conclusions from the data, and develop a position statement of *commendation* or *recommendation* for the school. The full report can be disseminated to the school principal and leadership council, district office, and community leaders.

References

Angelou, M. 1993. *On the pulse of morning*. New York: Random House.

Banks, J. A. 1990. Citizenship education for a pluralistic democratic society. *The Social Studies* 81(5): 210–14.

Banks, J. A. 1991–92. Multicultural education: For freedom's sake. *Educational Leadership* 49: 32–6.

Banks, J. A. 1993. Multicultural education: Characteristics and goals. In *Multicultural education: Issues and perspectives*, ed. J. A. Banks and C. A. M. Banks, 3–28. Boston: Allyn and Bacon.

Barber, B. R. 1992. *An aristocracy of everyone: The politics of education and the future of America*. New York: Ballantine Books.

Butts, R. F. 1978. *Public education in the United States: From revolution to reform*. New York: Holt, Rinehart and Winston.

Cagan, E. 1978. Individualism, collectivism, and radical educational reform. *Harvard Educational Review* 48(2): 227–66.

Cruse, H. 1987. *Plural but equal: A critical analysis of blacks and minorities and America's plural society*. New York: William Morrow and Company.

Darder, A. 1991. *Culture and power in the classroom: A critical foundation for bicultural education*. New York: Bergin and Garvey.

Davidman, L., and P. T. Davidman. 1994. *Teaching with a multicultural perspective: A practical guide*. New York: Longman.

Dewey, J. 1897. *My pedagogic creed*. New York: E. L. Kellogg and Co.

Dewey, J. 1916. *Democracy and education: An introduction to the philosophy of education*. New York: Macmillan.

Freire, P. 1980. *Education for critical consciousness*. New York: Continuum.

Giroux, H. A. 1992. *Border crossings: Cultural workers and the politics of education*. New York: Routledge.

Henry, W. A. 1990. Beyond the melting pot. *Time* 135 (April 9): 28–31.

Kohn, A. 1986. *No contest: The case against competition*. Boston: Houghton Mifflin.

Macdonald, J. B. 1977. Living democratically in schools: Cultural pluralism. In *Multicultural education: Commitments, issues and applications*, ed. C. A. Grant, 6–13. Washington, D.C.: Association for Supervision and Curriculum Development.

McElroy-Johnson, B. 1993. Giving voice to the voiceless. *Harvard Educational Review* 63(1): 85–104.

Morrison, T. 1992. *Playing in the dark: Whiteness and the literary imagination*. Cambridge: Harvard University Press.

Perry, T., and J. W. Fraser, eds. 1993. *Freedom's plow: Teaching in the multicultural classroom*. New York: Routledge.

Phenix, P. H. 1961. *Education and the common good: A moral philosophy of the curriculum*. New York: Harper and Brothers.

Ramirez, M., and A. Castañeda. 1974. *Cultural democracy, bicognitive development and education*. New York: Academic Press.

Shade, B. J., ed. 1989. *Culture, style, and the educative process*. Springfield, Ill.: Charles C. Thomas Publishers.

Sleeter, C. E., and C. A. Grant. 1988. *Making choices for multicultural education: Five approaches to race, class, and gender*. Columbus, Ohio.: Merrill Publishing Company.

Taba, H. 1962. *Curriculum development: Theory and practice*. New York: Harcourt, Brace and World.

Chapter 5

Pedagogical Principles

The professional judgments of the teacher should be based on an understanding of how the student's behavior and thought processes involve. . . the reenactment of cultural patterns. Being responsive . . . thus means to be aware of and capable of responding in educationally constructive ways to the ways in which cultural patterns influence the behavioral and mental ecology of the classroom.

(Bowers and Flinders 1990, xi)

Too frequently in the past, cultural characteristics [of ethnic background students] have caused these students to become alienated from schools with a predominantly Anglo culture. Now it is important to see ethnic characteristics as powerful resources for learning. . . . Rather than being denied in the classroom, they can and should be used to promote educational achievement.

(Burger 1973, 18)

From reading the preceding chapters, you have begun to anticipate issues that will be discussed and to plan how you will reflect on the ideas presented. If so, you have probably already begun to question your personal beliefs about how teaching and learning should proceed, how these processes should be adjusted to be more responsive to cultural diversity, and why you hold the beliefs you do. Perhaps you will pause here, and begin a journal of your thoughts on these questions. Write your reactions before you read the chapter, and then add other reflections as you read. At the end of the chapter, after you have made your last entry, review and reflect upon the journal to see if or when changes occurred in how you view teaching and learning in a culturally pluralistic society.

Another activity to help you create a "personal mindset" or framework for this chapter is the following prereading activity. Think about the ways you regularly alert your students to the kinds of knowledge and procedures that are important for successful learning in your classroom. For example, you might frequently use overhead transparencies to underscore key ideas, cue students to information on which they will be tested with comments like "keep this in mind" or "remember this," or use cooperative groups and peer tutoring as major components of your teaching style. Make a list of eight or ten of these practices and keep them nearby as you read through this chapter. It will also be helpful for you to do a *reflective review* of the list periodically—possibly after reading each section—to see if the discussions help you understand how and why the features of your teaching that you have identified are *culturally embedded*. The first reflective review of the list of your teaching procedures and priorities might be to group them into the five categories of teaching and learning principles discussed in this chapter.

A third chapter preview activity is to scan the topics to be discussed, and then design a set of interview questions to elicit educators' personal principles of teaching and learning related to the different topics. Some questions you may ask are: What is educational equity? Should Latino, Native American, Asian-American, and African-American students be treated the same as European-American students? How do you determine when students are ready to learn? Does this differ for mainstream European-American students and students of color? What obligations do teachers have toward students, other than teaching them their subject areas and skills? Use the list of questions you created to conduct a *self-interview*. Audiotape or videotape your interview and put it away until you finish reading this chapter.

This chapter is about how values and beliefs influence decisions about the structure and process of teaching and learning. The pedagogical principles they generate stem from two key questions and encompass both curriculum and instruction. One of the questions is about content. It asks, "What knowledge has the greatest worth for all students?" The other question is about methodology. It asks, "How can the educational process achieve maximum learning results for all students?" These questions, and the principles they generate, are essentially the same for general education and multicultural education. As is the case with principles of human development and socialization for democratic citizenship, the only difference is that multicultural education adds the contextual lens of cultural diversity to them. Thus, multicultural education asks: "What knowledge is of greatest worth for all students in a culturally pluralistic society?" and "What must we know about the relationship between cultural diversity and learning in order to make the educational process of maximum benefit for all students?" The questions are framed so as to incorporate the histories, cultures, experiences, and traditions of both majority and minority ethnic, racial, and social groups. This orientation is consistent with the idea that multicultural education includes everyone. Or, as some proponents claim, multicultural education is the *only* way to provide a relevant, appropriate, and quality education for a culturally pluralistic society such as that of the United States.

The discussion of the pedagogical principles included in this chapter is based on three major assumptions:

1. All teaching and learning are embedded in particular cultural contexts;

2. Cultural inconsistencies due to different expectations about knowledge and ways of knowing interfere with effective teaching and learning in culturally pluralistic classrooms; and

3. *Culturally responsive teaching* is an appropriate strategy for reforming classroom instruction, acceptable to both general and multicultural education.

Bowers and Flinders (1990) and Greenbaum (1985) found that most, if not all, of the important dimensions of knowledge and the procedures of teaching that we take for granted in schools are culturally determined. Bowers and Flinders (1990) identified several examples of "taken-for-granted" or "tacit" knowledge that are, in fact, culturally specific. They are: viewing time as linear, perceiving change as progressive, associating good things and success with spatial direction of "up" (e.g., "He's at the top of his field") and failure with "down" (e.g., "She is falling down in her grades"), and rationality as the best-quality thinking (e.g., "Your emotions are overshadowing your reasons"). Other examples include the following:

- Using a linear, three-part, topic-centered approach in telling stories (while some students are accustomed to a more circular, topic-chaining, episodic pattern of story telling).
- Using behavior patterns, such as pauses, eye contact, body gestures, and one-to-one communication, to establish the right to speaking turns (which may conflict with the more group-oriented patterns of some ethnic groups).
- Introducing new concepts by using metaphors that are limited to one gender, age, social class, ethnic, or cultural group.
- Representing numbers and facts as the best basis of high-quality thinking (when some students are more culturally inclined toward the authority of affective, relational, and aesthetic forms of knowledge).

- Giving priority to literate forms of discourse (while some students are embedded in various traditions of oral discourse) (Bowers and Flinders 1990).

These samples of "taken-for-granted knowledge" are included here to help create a general framework for the remainder of this chapter. This framework has two major pillars. One is the belief that if education is to fulfill its obligation of teaching well all children of the United States and making its other philosophical principles meaningful to everyone, then its content and processes must be multicultural. The other pillar is understanding that teaching as a *culturally relative process* has a profound impact upon how well educators are able to modify classroom dynamics to make them more sensitive and responsive to multiculturalism.

The number of pedagogical principles listed in Table 1.3 on page 24 is too extensive to discuss them all separately here. The same process was used to organize the discussion for this chapter as was applied in Chapters 3 and 4. The discussion is arranged according to 5 major themes embedded in and represented by the principles listed in Table 1.3. They are *universal literacy, scholarly truth, equity and excellence, developmental appropriateness, and teaching the whole child.*

Universal Literacy

General Principles:	Multicultural Translations:
• Education empowers through knowledge, morality, consciousness, and activism.	• Education empowers through knowledge, morality, consciousness, and activism about cultural diversity.
• All students should master basic literacy skills.	• Basic literacy skills should be learned within the context of cultural diversity.
• Critical-thinking and problem-solving skills are key components of quality education.	• Learning involves the application of critical thinking and problem solving to ethnic and cultural diversity issues.
• Education should prepare students for social responsibility.	• Education should teach skills to reform society to obtain equality, freedom, and justice for ethnically and culturally different groups.

General education and multicultural education agree that all students should be taught the fundamental knowledge and skills needed to function in an increasingly complex and globally interdependent society. All people need education to make the best of their membership in the human family, to exercise responsible conduct in social life, to make good choices, and to enhance their personal identities. Because the idea of democracy in the United States is founded upon an intelligent citizenry, "education should be universal, socially oriented, aimed at the development of mature judgment, and cognizant of individual differences" (Phenix 1961, 35). Basic literacy skills are the building blocks of this universal education.

Although the fundamental intellectual skills commonly referred to as the "three Rs" are central elements of literacy, educators are now saying that learning to read, write, and compute is not sufficient anymore for one to be considered literate. The complexities of contemporary and future life demand much more. The types of literacies people need to function well will multiply as society becomes more complex and the aspirations of individuals are raised. Arthur Combs (1991), the renowned humanistic psychologist, clarified some of these complexities and how they affect changing conceptions of literacy. He pointed out that we live in an extremely interdependent society. This interdependence makes us instantaneously visible and vulnerable to world audiences and events. Thanks to developments in electronic media, images of victims of war and famine ten thousand miles away are beamed into millions of homes in the United States as its citizens engage in their daily activities, surrounded by peaceful, safe, and secure neighborhoods. When historical rivalries among warring factions erupt in the Persian Gulf, we feel the effects immediately in the availability and costs of energy. The collapse of the Berlin Wall, the decline of the U.S.S.R., the ravages of war in Southeast Asia, and the economic and political difficulties in Haiti cause shifts in the ethnic distribution of our population at home. Other changes that have profound effects on how literacy is defined include the exponential growth of information, often called "the knowledge explosion"; the phenomenal pace of technological change; the primacy of "people problems" in the United States and the world; and the growing needs of individuals for personal affiliation and fulfillment in an increasingly crowded, violent, morally corrupt, and depersonalized society.

To accommodate these needs, current conceptions of literacy are adding myriad skills to the basic intellectual operations, including technological, geographic, scientific, global, religious, cultural, political, computer, economic, aesthetic, historical, and interpersonal competencies. Permeating all of these are companion process skills: critical thinking, problem solving, decision making, values clarification, conflict resolution, and social and political activism. These literacies are at once universal and particularistic. They are universal in that their value and utility apply to everyone. However, the specific forms of various literacies and the functions they serve for individuals, communities, and nations are as diverse as the historical, political, and cultural contexts in which they operate (Guthrie and Kirsch 1984).

Even though the list of what comprises literacy is expanding, the nature of the components remains essentially the same. The emphasis is more on process skills than factual content. Traditionally these have been understood within the framework of intellectual and cognitive operations, just as learning to read is a prerequisite for understanding mathematical propositions, extrapolating factual information from literary passages, comparing different perspectives on historical events, and analyzing scientific data. Now, notions of literacy are being extended to other areas of operation such as feelings, values, beliefs, morality, and social actions. Being literate also includes critically assessing knowledge content and sources; clarifying one's values about social and human rights issues; developing a sense of conscience and ethics as a guide for balancing commitments to technological and humanistic development; acting upon one's moral convictions to alleviate racial, cultural, social, and national prejudices, oppressions, and exploitations; and mastering skills of social and political action to change society and its institutions to be more egalitarian and accessible to all citizens.

What does multicultural education add to these conceptions of literacy? It offers specific operational frameworks for their application, and suggests an additional dimension or category of literacy. This is ethnic and cultural diversity, which has both content and context functions. A basic premise of multicultural education is that all students need to acquire more accurate knowledge about the cultures, histories, contributions, traditions, experiences, and critical events of the different ethnic, racial, and social groups which comprise the United States. This knowledge constitutes *ethnic literacy*. It is needed to compensate for the paucity of information that most people possess about their own and others' ethnic and cultural groups. Unfortunately, what many think is ethnic and cultural knowledge consists of stereotypes, distortions, and untruths, or, at best, partial truths. Lack of accurate information can lead to racial and ethnic fears and anxieties, as well as distorted levels of ethnocentricism and cultural biases. These attitudes, in turn, interfere with constructive relationships between people from different ethnic and cultural groups, and with the establishment of kinship and camaraderie.

These arguments are similar in kind and context to those provided by advocates of global and human relations literacies. The common implicit message is that U.S. students are not adequately prepared to be citizens of either national or global society since they lack the literacy component of culturally pluralistic knowledge and values.

Like other categories of competence, ethnic and cultural literacy encompasses more than factual information. Attitudes, values, and actions are also important. Students who are ethnically and culturally literate understand, respect, and appreciate how cultural diversity permeates their individual and social lives; they are actively involved in the cultivation and celebration of cultural diversity as a vital force for enriching future lives; and they exert their power and leverage in social and political situations to promote equality of treatment for all groups.

Ethnic and cultural literacy should be a *contextual factor* in all other learnings to which students are exposed. Other essential literacy skills can be practiced, and their mastery demonstrated, by using culturally different materials, experiences, examples, and perspectives. Reading, writing, critical thinking, and problem-solving have no substantive content of their own. They are *intellectual processes* that rely on some other substantive sources for their application. People do not "read" reading or use critical thinking to do critical thinking; instead they apply reading, thinking, and problem-solving skills to some other database. Invariably, these substantive sources derive from the social settings, cultures, and times in which schools exist. Since cultural diversity is a definitive feature of U.S. and world cultures, material related to it is appropriate and vital to use in teaching these process skills. Thus, students can practice critical thinking by investigating the allocation of economic resources among ethnic groups in the United States. They can learn vocabulary, word attack, and inference skills by reading poems, essays, short stories, and speeches written by individuals from different ethnic, racial, and gender groups. Mathematical concepts and operations such as proportion, distribution, projections, and percentages can be practiced by using actual information about ethnic groups' immigration rates, employment trends, settlement locations throughout the country, and enrollment patterns in schools, colleges and universities.

Multiple benefits result from integrating ethnic and cultural literacy into other types of literacies. First, multicultural education and generic intellectual skills are taught simultaneously, and the two reinforce each other. Second, the interest appeal of the materials used to teach skills increases and, in turn, causes a corresponding improvement in the relevance, depth, and transfer of learning for more students. Third, the importance of cultural and ethnic literacy for all students is demonstrated by attaching it to other high status educational priorities. Fourth, the idea that quality education for U.S. students and society is necessarily multicultural becomes institutionalized and a regular part of the daily operations of the instructional process. Fifth, the commitment of schools to making education successful for all children may come closer to being realized when general education priorities are processed through many different cultural filters.

Scholarly Truth

General Principles:	Multicultural Translations:
• Education content and process should include the contributions of everyone.	• Education content and processes should incorporate culturally pluralistic contributions.
• Education should transmit the cumulative knowledge of humankind and the national culture.	• Culturally different groups have contributed to the cumulative knowledge of humankind and of the national culture.
• Search for truth is a valid educational goal.	• Genuine search for truth is valid only if it includes cultural pluralism.
• Knowledge is cultural capital.	• Culturally pluralistic knowledge has greater cultural capital value than monocultural knowledge.

Of importance equal to that of universal literacy in conventional U.S. educational thinking is the idea that all students have a right to knowledge that is accurate. Many U.S. educators believe that intellectual liberation can be achieved by knowing "the truth." The basis used to establish this "truth" is the presumed claim of objectivity and rationality attached to scientific inquiry: If a statement can be verified with quantitative facts, then it is almost certainly "absolute truth" because "facts don't lie." Hence, mainstream education assigns more value and importance to reason than intuition, to cognition than emotion, and to scientific knowledge than aesthetics.

These beliefs are often signified by two common axioms: "The truth shall set you free" and "Knowledge is power." Individuals who have knowledge—that is, mastery of a body of *verifiable* facts—are better able to think for themselves, critically analyze various interpretations of events, defend their moral convictions, and make their own decisions without being unduly influenced or intimidated by others. They are empowered for personal autonomy, and for heightened social responsibility. Phenix (1961) believed that these skills lead to the improvement of both social democracy and individual humanity.

Multicultural education dethrones any single source of authority and opens the gateway for knowledge to find expression in many different forms and sources. It suggests that knowledge and scholarly truth in a culturally pluralistic society are relative, and socially constructed. Different individuals and groups have very different notions of what comprises knowledge and truth; their perceptions reflect their social, cultural, and ethnic experiences. For example, a government document may present one version of "truth" about the internment of Japanese-Americans during World War II by giving a numerical analysis of how many and to where individuals from different cities were relocated. Japanese-Americans who describe life before, during, and after the internment give an entirely different version of knowledge and truth. Which one is correct? Mainstream education may say the government report is better because it is dispassionate and deals only with numbers. But is it really dispassionate, since it is delivered from the vantage point of a mainstream cultural value (e.g., high priority given to cognition and quantifiable sources of knowledge) and presented in a way that serves a particular historical viewpoint, purpose, and audience? Multicultural education endorses the validity of both in that the Japanese-American and traditional historical accounts provide different perspectives on the same event. It also supports the idea that the Japanese-American perspective is just as legitimate as the government's. Depending on the purpose and intent, this perspective may be even more important. The point is that each party is actively engaged in creating knowledge about the same event. While both may be legitimate and valid, they are also *relative*.

Multiculturalists suggest that, contrary to the common misconception held by many educators, truth is never totally objective, absolute, and permanent. Instead, the quest for knowledge and truth is a continuing process, and a universal feature of humanity. Everyone does it. However, just as there is no one model American or human being, no single group has a monopoly on knowledge, and there is no one universal canon of truth that is equally valid for everyone. Consider how perceptions of events change as new information and discoveries emerge. For many years, people wrote convincingly about how enslaved Africans in the U.S. passively appealed to religion for redemption from their fate. Recent analyses of their religious practices and songs now suggest that they engaged in what Cone (1984) called a "theology of liberation." Many of the religious songs were coded messages of resistance and opposition to oppression. Phenix (1961, 35–36) reminded us that "knowledge is never purely objective, nor purely subjective, but a product of object-subject relationships. . . . Knowledge is hypothetical and conditional rather than absolute, in the sense that any true statement is an assertion about what is the case under certain specified circumstances of observing, experimenting, and language usage." Therefore, in a genuine search for truth, no prescriptions of knowledge are used to impose arbitrary limitations on inquiry, inquiry proceeds freely without any form of coercion, and no obstacles are created to prevent the truth from being heard. Furthermore, "the many kinds of knowledge and the wide variety of symbolic forms by which it may be expressed and mediated should be acknowledged and utilized" (Phenix 1961, 42).

Phenix's comments on the nature of knowledge and truth strike a responsive chord among multiculturalists. They suggest that many complex factors influence what becomes knowledge and truth for different individuals and groups, and how that truth is expressed. Some of these factors are the actual occurrence, the interpretations attached to the experience, the ethnic identity, social context, and cultural backgrounds of the interpreters, and their positions in the economic and political structures of society (Banks, 1993b).

There is no question that slavery existed in the United States, but "truths" about that existence vary greatly. Slave owners, abolitionists, enslaved Africans, nineteenth-century mainstream historians, and African-American social psychologists all relate different versions of the experience. The medium used to record and share experiences also influences what is told and how well. Poetry, personal narrations, fictionalized accounts, interpretative essays, newspaper reports, and biographical renditions offer different perspectives on slavery. To a degree, all of them represent both truth and untruth. As students examine different versions of the "truth" of various critical incidents, events, and developments in U. S. history, life, and culture, they will begin to experience what some educators (Darder 1991; Giroux 1988, 1992; Shor 1992; Sleeter 1991; Suzuki 1984) mean by *knowledge is socially constructed, curriculum transformation, deconstructing existing knowledge paradigms,* and *being actively involved in the creation of one's own knowledge.*

The diversity of knowledge sources, and the corresponding interpretations or truths they generate, must be made accessible to students in U.S. schools as part of teaching them how to live effectively in society and to fully appreciate the gifts of humankind. This knowledge will help remind them that "human culture is the product of the struggles of all humanity, not the possession of a single racial or ethnic group" (Hilliard 1991–92, 13). The intent of having students critically examine these struggles and the knowledge they produce is not to find a single, definitive, absolute truth, but to ensure that <u>all</u> perspectives central to issues and experiences are examined thoroughly and thoughtfully. This means that any valid canon of knowledge is inherently culturally pluralistic. It attests to the power of Hilliard's (1991–92) statement that the multicultural goal of pluralizing school curricula is not a matter of using ethnic quotas to balance perspectives, or replacing one cultural standard of truth with another; instead, it is simply a question of teaching knowledge with accuracy and validity.

As students continue the struggle to understand the legacy of humankind and its many sources, they will become active constructors and more thoughtful consumers of knowledge. They will also be more capable of formulating their own knowledge about ethnic and cultural diversity, and scrutinizing other claims of truth for their accuracy and validity (Banks 1990). Hence, understanding the knowledge construction process is a critical form of intellectual, personal, and social power for students, embedded in principles of teaching and learning for both general and multicultural education.

Equity and Excellence

General Principles:	Multicultural Translations:
• Cooperative and collaborative learning has positive academic and social effects.	• Effective education shows how cultural groups are interrelated.
• Equity and excellence are moral imperatives of education.	• Equity and excellence are impossible without sensitivity to cultural diversity.
• Self-concepts and academic achievement are interrelated.	• Positive ethnic identities have positive effects on the academic achievement of culturally diverse students.

In order for all students to experience educational *excellence,* there must be *equity* of access, resources, content, and processes. Multicultural education places these notions within the framework of cultural diversity by explaining that educational programs that do not include cultural pluralism as a central feature can never be considered excellent. Nor can students from different ethnic groups and cultural backgrounds have a real chance to achieve educational excellence without equity in the learning system. Implicit in these beliefs are conceptions of excellence and equity that are much broader than the conventional focus on academic achievement and equal treatment. Excellence must include all dimensions of learning the cognitive, social, psychological, emotional, interpersonal, moral, and aesthetic. Similarly, equity requires much more than providing similar treatment to students who differ in significant ways. A case in point is learning styles. Using the same techniques and procedures to teach students who learn in different ways ensures inequity of learning opportunities and outcomes.

Thus, both excellence and equity are required if either is to be achieved. For this relationship to be clearly understood and implemented, some common misconceptions need to be eliminated. Montero-Sieburth (1988) provided a helpful perspective. She explained that the concept of equity is historically grounded in the democratic principle of equal education for equal participation. Unfortunately, in practice, equity initiatives have been governed by the assumption of homogeneity—the belief that educational equity can be guaranteed by providing the same kind of education for all students, regardless of their individual ethnic, racial, or cultural differences. Many educators believe that if they do not treat all students identically, they are being discriminatory and inequitable.

Multicultural education challenges both assumptions: that being responsive to individual and cultural differences among students is discrimination, and that equity is synonymous with sameness. Gay (1988, 328) explained a more appropriate relationship between equity and excellence for improving the quality of teaching and learning in a pluralistic setting:

> *Whereas equity is a methodological input issue, excellence is an evaluative outcome measure. Excellence finds expression in common standards and expectations of high achievement for all students, and equity translates into appropriate methodologies and materials according to specific group and individual characteristics. Excellence occurs when individual students achieve to the best of their ability, and equity is accomplished when each student is provided with learning opportunities that make high level achievement possible. . . . If learners from different ethnic, social, and cultural groups do not have access to comparable quality resources, facilities, and instructional interactions as others who are succeeding in school, then their chances for achieving excellence are minimized.*

Access to high-quality, high-status knowledge is necessary for educational excellence, but does not guarantee it; nor does the belief that all students can learn. These are two popular dicta of the most current school reform and effectiveness movements. Multiculturalists contend that, in practice, no students can enjoy the best educational opportunities possible or learn as well as they might, unless all learning experiences are comparable—not identical—in quality and kind. Since all children do not learn in the same ways, they cannot learn to the best of their ability if they are treated identically in the instructional process. *How* students learn, as well as *what* they learn, are functions of their ethnic identity, social class, and cultural backgrounds. Teacher attitudes, expectations, and competence, instructional materials and techniques, and school and classroom climates also affect what kind of learning experiences students from various ethnic and cultural backgrounds receive. All of these are critical factors in providing educational equity and excellence for all students.

The essence of instructional equity is the use of comparable but diverse strategies to accomplish common achievement outcomes for culturally different students. "The emphasis is on quality status, significance of learning opportunities, and equivalency of effect potential (having similar likelihood of producing similar kinds of results). Since these will vary by circumstance, purpose, group, and individual, the best way to achieve comparability of learning opportunities is to differentiate among them according to the characteristics of the students for whom they are intended" (Gay 1988, 329). The roles of A. Philip Randolph in organizing the Brotherhood of Sleeping Car Porters, Cesar Chavez in forming the United Farmers Workers Organization, and Samuel Gompers in creating the American Federation of Labor are comparable examples of the leadership of an African-American, a Mexican-American, and a European-American, respectively, in the labor union movement. The message here is similar in intent and technique to that of some civic leaders whose motto is "by any means necessary" to eliminate inequities in social, political, and economic opportunities. Another symbolic summary of these instructional priorities is Asante's (1991–92) notion that achieving plurality without hierarchy is both the means and ends of incorporating cultural diversity in all components of the educational process. That is, teaching students that many different ethnic and cultural groups have made valuable contributions to the shaping of U.S. life and that major issues and events in society are better understood when analyzed from many different perspectives.

If educators are to provide comparable learning opportunities for culturally different students, they need to understand specific cultural characteristics of ethnic, racial, and social groups, and how culture shapes the behaviors of teachers and students in learning situations. Instructional strategies should then be designed to *reflect and complement* these styles and preferences (García 1982; Gay 1988; Hale-Benson 1986; Shade 1989). This does not mean that teachers should know everything about every ethnic group. Such an expectation is unreasonable and impossible. But, teachers do need an understanding of key cultural traits and core values of major ethnic groups in the United States. They also need to know (1) how to recognize cultural differences in their students; (2) how to ask informative questions about cultural diversity; (3) how to involve students actively in the process of accumulating useful cultural information about different groups; and (4) how and why diverse techniques such as individual competition, cooperative groups, visual learning, peer tutoring, and participatory learning are needed to ensure that students who learn in different ways have comparable opportunities to master learning tasks. By providing more options for how students can approach learning tasks, none will be unduly advantaged or disadvantaged in the procedural aspects of learning. This point is crucial in making provisions for educational excellence.

A growing body of educational research and scholarship (see, for example, Boykin 1986; Kochman 1981; Shade 1989; Spindler 1987; and Cazden, John, and Hymes 1985) suggests that some of the more serious problems students of color have with academic achievement are matters of mismatches in the procedures of teaching and learning rather than lack of intellectual ability, interest, or motivation. These observations led Holliday (1985) to conclude that competence in, and successful adaptation to, the social and procedural rules of schooling are prerequisites for academic success. If students violate the rules of turn-taking in the classroom, they have less opportunity to participate in the content of teaching and learning. Some children are denied the chance to read, or contribute their ideas to a discussion, because they do not raise their hand or wait to be called on. Raising the hand is a *management or procedural rule,* while reading and contributing ideas to discussions are *substantive components* of teaching and learning. Other more subtle behaviors, such as personal hygiene habits, nonverbal communication nuances, and dialects and accents have as much, if not more, effect on the kind of opportunities offered students from various ethnic and cultural backgrounds to participate in instructional interactions in the classroom. Therefore, providing educational equity and excellence for culturally pluralistic students has substantive, procedural, instructional, environmental, and interactional components (Montero-Sieburth 1988). They, like other dimensions of multicultural education, require comprehensive, holistic, and systemic institutional and individual reform. As Montero-Sieburth (1988, 131) cautions, "In analyzing how equity is achieved it is crucial that we consider multiple factors and their interactive power to create positive learning opportunities."

Developmental Appropriateness

General Principles:	Multicultural Translations:
• Continuity across learning experiences improves achievement levels.	• Teaching styles should be accepting of different cultural learning styles.
• Child-centered learning is most effective.	• Understanding cultural traits of students makes teaching more effective.
• Education strategies should be compatible with the readiness levels of students.	• Ethnic and cultural factors should be used in determining students' readiness for learning.
• Intrinsic motivation leads to greater learning.	• Some motivation for learning is culture-specific.

Closely related to the idea of making educational opportunities equitable and excellent for all students is the principle that students learn better when instructional tasks and techniques are appropriate for their ability levels and learning styles. This is called the *developmental appropriateness* of teaching and learning. It is one of the key conditions or criteria of educational equity.

This principle of learning yields several implications for analysis and practice, including *readiness, continuity, compatibility, pacing,* and *validity*. In theory, it means that all components of the content, context, and process of learning are determined by, and in agreement with, the profile of individual learners. It is another way of conceptualizing the idea that the child is the beginning, center, and end of all instructional decisions and actions. In practice, educators tend to use group patterns and developmental trends, and depend most heavily on intellectual development to guide instructional planning and practice.

Multicultural education is based on the belief that understanding both the individual and cultural characteristics of students is essential to making educational practices more developmentally appropriate for all students. This notion was developed further by Brembeck and Hill (1973) in their explanations of the relationship between culture and learning. They contended that cultural characteristics are (1) as much a part of individuals' personal endowments and learning potentials as are psychological characteristics; (2) persistent and continuous over time; and (3) as available for and significant to the improvement of teaching and learning as psychological traits.

Readiness for learning is one of the most common criteria educators use to determine the developmental appropriateness of instruction. It can be defined as the psycho-emotional disposition and ability of individuals that make them receptive to learning. It is based on the assumption that effective learning requires educational experiences to be closely aligned with the developmental sequences and levels of growth in individuals.

Two ideas are particularly significant for designing instructional programs and practices to match the readiness levels of students: (1) the development process becomes increasingly more complex across the life span of the school-age years, and (2) the various aspects of development (physical, social, emotional, intellectual, moral, cultural) are closely interrelated. These ideas suggest that teaching and learning should increase in complexity and sophistication as the school years advance, to parallel the natural order of human development. Learning should proceed sequentially from simple to complex, from concrete to abstract, from present to past, from self-centered to other-centered, from the tangible and tactile to the hypothetical and ideational, from acquiring information to critically analyzing its sources, purposes, and validity. A good illustration of these orientations is the cognitive Taxonomy of Educational Objectives (Bloom, Engelhart, Furst, Hill, and Krathwohl 1956). It organizes intellectual skills in a increasingly complex and sophisticated sequence, starting with *knowledge* and progressing through *comprehension, application, analysis, synthesis,* and *evaluation.* These perceptions of how to sequence teaching and learning reflect the linear emphasis of mainstream cultural values and rules about how to organize human interactions, and are not sensitive to the research that suggests that many ethnic and cultural groups do not ascribe to the same values, rules, and priorities.

Unfortunately, many educators continue to rely heavily upon either mental indicators, as measured by Piaget's stages of intellectual development, or physical levels of motor skills development, to determine students' readiness for learning. They believe that students who are in the formal operations phase of the Piagetian model are more capable of sophisticated and abstract learning than those in the sensorimotor and concrete stages. Such students are ready to engage in problem solving using hypothetical situations; to empathize with the situations and circumstances of others outside their immediate environment; to apply ethical standards in governing behavior; and to use higher-order thinking skills such as analysis, synthesis, and evaluation. The content of different subjects is organized in a similar pattern. Percentages, ratios, and pre-algebra can be taught in seventh-grade mathematics because the basic operations of adding, subtracting, dividing, and multiplying have been mastered in the lower grades. Students can be expected to write well-crafted compositions only after they have learned the basic rules of grammar. Some recent pedagogical developments suggest that we may be moving away from strict adherence to linear patterns of teaching and learning. These include instructional techniques such as reading and writing across the curriculum, whole language learning, integrated curriculum, interdisciplinary team teaching, and cooperative learning.

Overreliance on any single dimension of development to assess readiness for learning is too narrow a basis for making crucial instructional decisions that shape students' entire learning careers. It is also in direct contradiction to the diversity inherent in the human condition, and the cultural socialization of students in the United States. Taba (1962, 95) explained why:

> *If each aspect of . . . development is contingent on another, a proper prediction of what a student can or cannot do should not be made without examining all [of its] significant dimensions. . . . The evidence on interrelationship among the several aspects of growth also suggests that each individual brings to each learning situation a differentiated combination of capacities and abilities, each at a particular level of maturity. This would indicate that readiness to learn is determined by such a constellation rather than by any single individual factor. Diagnosis,*

then, should attempt to describe these constellations of
developmental patterns and the factors affecting them.

Multiculturalists agree wholeheartedly with Taba's conception of readiness for learning and its application in teaching culturally different students. They consider readiness to be the intellectual *and* psychosocial predisposition of students to receive, process, and understand learning stimuli. Intellectual ability provides the rudimentary potential for being receptive to and capable of learning. Whether and how this is actualized in behavior is affected by a combination of personal, cultural, and situational factors. Significant among these are teacher attitudes and expectations, the nature of the school and community climates in which learning occurs, the relevance and interest appeal of the materials and resources used in teaching, and the overall feeling of well-being of students. All of these, in turn, are influenced by ethnic and racial identity, social class, and cultural conditioning (Cazden, John, and Hymes 1985; García 1982; Nieto 1992).

Several examples illustrate how issues specific to cultural diversity affect the learning readiness of students. First, many students from different ethnic groups, social classes, and cultural backgrounds feel alienated, discriminated against, and insignificant in schools. These feelings cut across gender, achievement levels, and school settings. In other words, it is not only poor students of color living in large cities and failing in school who have these feelings. Achieving, middle-class European-American students living in suburban communities do not find school very exciting, supportive, and embracing either. In his extensive study, *A Place Called School,* John Goodlad (1984) provided a graphic and chilling account of what life is like in most schools, substantiating students' perceptions. These feelings are not conducive to high-level academic performance, even though students may be very capable intellectually. Similarly, instructional materials that ignore or demean certain ethnic groups and cultural traditions can become impenetrable obstacles to learning for students from those backgrounds. Developmentally appropriate instructional practices reduce the likelihood of these situations occurring because they incorporate knowledge about and sensitivity to factors of race, ethnicity, social class, and culture, and how they affect learning behaviors.

Second, classroom practices can be made more responsive to the learning readiness levels of culturally different students by matching them with the stages of ethnic identity development discussed in Chapter 3. Students who are ashamed or unconscious of their ethnicity have a different level of readiness for learning about their own and others' cultures from those who are proud of their ethnic identity. They may resist and reject all classroom efforts to celebrate cultural diversity. Students who are comfortable with their ethnicity may be eager, excited, and very willing to share their own, and learn about others' cultural heritages, traditions, and experiences. These different stages of ethnic identification should be considered in designing strategies to teach other skills and subjects such as reading, math, and science, since positive self-concept, cultural consciousness, and level of ethnic identity correlate positively with academic efforts and achievement (Phinney and Traver 1988; Streitmatter 1989).

A third readiness question concerns what and how to teach students about issues central to multicultural education. For example, all proponents agree that racism is a crucial issue that needs to be addressed in all multicultural education programs. But how is it possible to teach about racism in ways that are appropriate and authentic for first-graders, as well as fifth-, tenth-, and twelfth-graders? How can constructive teaching and learning about racism proceed without drifting into "White bashing" and "guilt tripping"? General education would look primarily at the intellectual maturity of students to answer these questions. Multicultural education says this is not enough to adequately determine students' readiness for dealing with racism. Other significant factors must be considered as well, such as the racial and ethnic composition of the classroom, the students' prior experiences with racism, the kinds of racist practices to which their ethnic groups have been subjected, the racial climate of the school and classroom, and the level of teacher competence and confidence.

A fourth prominent theme in multicultural education is the need to provide students with a variety of different ethnic and cultural role models. The choice of likely candidates to serve this function should be influenced by the students' intellectual levels, emotional, social, cultural consciousness, and ethnic identity development. The same individuals who captivate third-grade Latinos may be rejected by seventh- or eleventh-graders. Students who are caught in the midst of clarifying their ethnic identity may find those who are not members of their own ethnic group—or members who seem to interact too closely with ethnic others—unacceptable as role models. A proponent of integration may be perceived as a "sell-out" to his or her own group. To other students, these types of individuals are prototypes of the most desirable values and behaviors in a culturally pluralistic society. Hence, African-Americans who are just beginning to come to terms with their ethnicity may eagerly welcome Malcolm X as a role model but reject Booker T. Washington. Those who have completed the process may accept both, as well as individuals from other cultural groups. The discussion of stages of human growth and ethnic identity development in Chapter 3 explain some reasons for variations in reactions to instructional methods and materials.

A fifth readiness question deals with the institutional climate of schools and classrooms. Multicultural educators believe that programs and practices related to cultural pluralism should be compatible with the environmental context in which students live and learn. As with individuals, the readiness levels or receptivity of schools and communities for multicultural education vary. Programs for and about cultural diversity should be responsive to this variance. In schools where there is a lot of interracial hostility, focus on prejudice reduction may be far more appropriate than concentration on cross-cultural interactions. Schools and neighborhoods where ethnic and racial diversity is a new occurrence may benefit more from basic knowledge of cultural characteristics and artifacts, and ethnic myths and stereotypes, than from trying to achieve empathy from students for victims of cultural and racial oppression. Schools with a single ethnic group of color (such as African-Americans, Asian-Americans, or Latinos) will require different strategies to teach common multicultural issues from schools with mostly European-American students or multiracial populations. The intent of these different instructional emphases is to accommodate different developmental levels of schools and classrooms, not to suggest that multicultural education is more or less important for some students and institutional settings than others.

Several multiculturalists (Baker 1983; Banks 1993a; Baptiste 1986; Bennett 1990; Gibson 1976; Nieto 1992; Sleeter and Grant 1988) have designed models that can be helpful in matching appropriate multicultural curricular and instructional practices to the developmental readiness levels of students, teachers, and schools. Typically, the models progress from supplementing regular course content, lessons, and units with ethnic contributions; to infusing cultural diversity into all parts of curriculum and instruction; to transforming the structures of the entire educational enterprise to reflect cultural pluralism; to developing social consciousness, moral convictions, and political action skills needed to promote equality, freedom, and justice in schools and society.

Continuity is another significant condition of developmentally appropriate instruction. It is endorsed by both general education and multicultural education, and means that instructional strategies and learning experiences that build upon the knowledge bases, learning styles, and frames of reference of students are likely to be more effective than those that abruptly introduce change. This idea is expressed by educators when they declare that the teaching process should "start where children are" and expand their horizons afterwards. Many multicultural education beliefs parallel this philosophy. One is the idea that students should be affirmed and validated in their own cultural frames of reference before they are expected to engage in cultural reform. Another belief is that students should be taught how to shift from one cultural style of operating to others to fit situational needs, as part of the skills required for school success and living in a culturally pluralistic society (Holliday 1985; Shade 1989). Gay (1993) suggested a third multicultural education interpretation of establishing continuity in learning—"building cultural bridges" between the different styles of learning, behaving, valuing, relating, and communicating that students encounter at home and at school.

Long before multicultural education became a prominent issue, Taba (1962) analyzed why continuity between the home and school is so important to students' success. She observed that the rules, expectations, and procedures required to succeed in school constitute a whole new value system and *modus operandi* for students from cultural groups different from those that set the norms in schools. Conflicts often result, with negative effects on academic achievement. They are compounded by social class, race, ethnic, and language differences, by the failure of school programs to bridge these cultural gaps, by curriculum content that has little practical meaning to the lives of some students, and by instructional techniques that do not reflect the ways students are accustomed to learning in their home cultures. Consequently, for many students:

*The school itself is a contributing agent to some of the
difficulties in learning. It creates nonlearners by systematically alienating a substantial portion of . . . youth, not
all of whom are individuals of inferior ability. . . . Since
there is no scientific reason for assuming . . . that talent is
more scarce among lower-class and minority groups, the
explanation of differences in achievement and the
functioning of learning ability among these groups must
be found in the conflict between the content of social
learning and the content of the curriculum, and in the
discrepancies between the motivational devices that the
school uses and the actual motivation. . . . It seems, then,
that it is important for educators to consider the conflicts
and discontinuities involved in adjustment to school
culture. . . . Modification of curricula and of methods to
help close the gap between social learning and the school
culture might be the key to opening avenues to learning
for many more students* (Taba 1962, 146–47).

This line of analysis continues in multicultural education. Examples were
provided by Holliday (1985), Irvine (1990), McDermott (1987), Nieto (1992),
and Shade and New (1993), who noted that major communication and interaction barriers can exist between some culturally diverse students and their
teachers. These are caused by differing expectations about acceptable behavior, social decorum, procedural rules, and communication content, form, and
style. These discrepancies have negative effects on learning motivation, efforts,
and outcomes. To reverse these trends and improve academic success for
greater numbers of culturally diverse students, teachers should foster classroom climates and use instructional techniques that facilitate a wide variety of
relational, communication, thinking, and learning styles.

Two strategies emerge from multicultural education theory for creating
cultural bridges and continuity in learning and for making the educational
process more inviting for culturally diverse students. They are *matching
teaching styles with culturally different learning styles,* and *promoting cultural
context teaching*. Paulo Freire's (1992) *Pedagogy of the Oppressed,* which

resulted from his work with impoverished Brazilians, is often quoted in support of these ideas. The philosophy and research of King and Wilson (1990), Ladson-Billings and Henry (1990), Foster (1989), and Shade (1989) provide additional support for *culturally relevant* approaches to teaching, or anchoring the instructional process in the students' own cultural and experiential backgrounds.

Essentially, these teaching strategies use the contributions, experiences, and perspectives of diverse groups to make learning more relevant and valid. For students who incline toward kinesthetic learning, teachers should center much of the instruction in motion and movement activities. Individuals from cultural backgrounds that give high priority to group and communal efforts in task performance may perform better in cooperative and collaborative learning formats. Learning activities grounded in social issues, affective experiences, and participatory and discovery learning are a better match for students from cultures that place a high value on interpersonal relations and demonstrating abilities in performance behaviors.

In order to match instructional and learning styles, teachers must be familiar with the preferred learning modalities of individual students, and understand how these are affected by culture and ethnicity. Barbe and Swassing (1979) provided helpful descriptions of learning modalities (verbal, visual, auditory, tactile, kinesthetic) and the kinds of instructional strategies most appropriate for each, but these are not culturally specific. Multicultural education suggests ways these general learning preferences can and should be translated to apply to different cultural groups. This is necessary because culture and ethnicity have a strong impact on shaping learning styles. Therefore, teachers must understand cultural characteristics of different ethnic, racial, and social groups so they can develop instructional practices that are more responsive to cultural pluralism. Cultural characteristics of particular significance in this undertaking are communication styles, thinking styles, value systems, socialization processes, relational patterns, and performance styles (Bennett 1990; Hale-Benson 1986; Shade 1989; Shade and New 1993).

Throughout the process of making educational programs and practices more developmentally appropriate by matching teaching and learning styles, teachers should keep in mind four points:

1. Learning styles are multidimensional, fluid, individually and culturally determined, and, to some degree, situational.

2. Gender may have a significant influence on learning styles. Research suggests that males and females, within and across ethnic and cultural groups, have some unique learning style characteristics (Gilligan 1982; Halpern 1986).

3. In addition to the perceptual orientation described by Barbe and Swassing (1979), other key components of learning styles are environmental setting, substantive content, motivation, procedural preferences, and interpersonal qualities.

4. Some of the learning style components are stable across time and context, while others vary greatly. Once basic learning patterns are established they tend to prevail thereafter as the *primary points of reference and central tendencies* for processing information, thinking, and problem solving. Students enter into the learning process through their preferred styles, but they do not always operate exclusively in a single learning style (Kochman 1981; Shade 1989). It is also possible for students to learn how to operate effectively in different learning styles—that is, how to "style shift."

Most assuredly, matching teaching styles with culturally different learning styles offers many promising opportunities for establishing cultural continuity and developmental appropriateness in the instructional process, thereby improving learning for diverse students. These may be achieved by modifying how students are organized for learning, and the relationships between students and teachers, as well as by changing the content of instruction and the ways in which performance is evaluated. Ramirez and Castañeda (1974), Shade (1989), Hale-Benson (1986), Kochman (1981), and Cazden, John, and Hymes (1985) provided more extensive descriptions of the learning styles of different ethnic and cultural groups. These are valuable resources to assist teachers in adapting their instructional styles to better accommodate and incorporate cultural diversity.

Classroom instruction can be further culturally contextualized by using a variety of culturally pluralistic examples, scenarios, and vignettes for learners to practice and demonstrate mastery of concepts, facts, and skills. Novels written by individuals from different ethnic and cultural groups can be used to illustrate the mechanics of fiction writing such as plot, setting, character development, theme, and climax. Ethnic-group, social-class, and gender vernacular can be used to illustrate the concept of "voice" and contextual meanings. Economic principles of supply and demand can be demonstrated with data about patterns of ethnic employment and consumerism. The point of these suggestions is that culture is a powerful screen through which abstract phenomena and new learning experiences can be filtered to make them more meaningful to different students. This is the essence of cultural context teaching. It is a valuable tool for improving academic achievement and for demonstrating the reciprocal relationship between educational quality, equity, and excellence.

Teaching the Whole Child

General Principles:	Multicultural Translations:
• Education should expand the horizons of all children.	• Students should be taught cultural style-shifting skills.
• Education should maximize the individual potential of students.	• Educational programs and practices should be sensitive to how culture and ethnicity influence the academic, social, and psychological potential of students.
• The abilities of students should be measured against their own standards.	• Educators should understand that many individual competencies and skills are culturally contextual and situationally specific.

Another principle of general and multicultural education that is closely connected to achieving educational excellence and developmental appropriateness is teaching the whole child. This principle is based on the belief that true education encompasses more than developing the intellectual ability of students. Good, high-quality education is a holistic process in that knowledge, attitudes, values, morality, ethics, and actions are developed simultaneously. This is true for both personal growth and social development, especially within the philosophy of democratic citizenship and individual self-actualization.

Whether we realize it or not, most learning activities involve the student at multiple levels. A rather simple drill on geographic concepts, a minor chemical experiment, and a short, straightforward, reflective, free-writing assignment are not as isolated and fragmented as they may first appear. What seem like simple cognitive tasks are emotionally, psychologically, and culturally engaging as well. They involve positive and negative reactions to the teacher's expectations and instructional styles, the attitudes of other students in the classroom, social memories, aesthetic values, and ethnic and cultural identity. "In this sense learning concerns the whole person and results in an entire reorganization of the individual's pattern of behavior" (Thorpe and Schmuller 1954, 461).

Foshay (1975) identified six essential dimensions of the human condition that must be nurtured routinely in the educational process if educators are to teach the whole child. These are the intellectual, the physical, the aesthetic, the spiritual, the emotional, and the social. Other variations of this idea were discussed earlier in relation to the principles of human growth and development and the interaction between individual and social development. More contemporary interpretations appear as proposals for *integrated curriculum,* where content and concepts from different subject areas are taught in conjunction so that learning becomes a unified, rather than a fragmented, experience.

The importance of teaching the whole child is supported by the belief that developing any single aspect of a student's capabilities succeeds to the degree that all others are cultivated. Cultivating some and ignoring others creates an imbalance that contradicts the imperative of maximizing human potential. For example, emotional blocks can prevent learning as effectively as lack of mental ability, just as a sense of psychological well-being can enhance academic performance.

Multicultural education helps classroom teachers and school administrators understand what teaching the whole child means for culturally different students. Whereas Dewey saw the child as the beginning, center, and end of all educational decision making, multiculturalists suggest that children must always be centered in their culture and ethnicity to find both their individuality and their human universality. Educational programs and instructional practices designed for them must be similarly grounded. African-American, Asian-American, Latino, European-American, and Native American students can never maximize their human potential if the cultural and ethnic components of their humanity are ignored in the educational process (Asante 1991–92; García 1982). In addition to being of major importance as separate factors, these variables permeate all other aspects of the human condition—intellectual, social, psychological, physical, moral, ethical, or aesthetic. The goal of creating a "safe" environment in schools, where all children can learn, is unattainable without addressing cultural and ethnic factors. Ensuring that every child leaves school having mastered basic literacy skills cannot be accomplished without simultaneously attending to their cultural consciousness, moral character, and ethnic identity.

The commitment to teaching the whole child is embedded in all principles, concepts, and strategies of multicultural education. However, it is transmitted especially through the ideas of *infusion* and *systemic change.* Proponents of multicultural education contend that because cultural pluralism is holistic in that it characterizes all dimensions of the human condition, changes in educational programs and practices designed to respond to this diversity also must be *systemic* and *pervasive.* All parts of the schooling process must be culturally pluralized—policy mandates; formal and informal curricula; instructional methods and materials; institutional climate, values, symbols, and ethos; administrative leadership; counseling and guidance; and diagnosis of needs and performance assessment (Banks and Banks 1993; Bennett 1990; Hernandez 1989; Nieto 1992).

These changes are too comprehensive and multidimensional to be the responsibility of only one or a few aspects of the educational enterprise. Sometimes the affirmation and celebration of cultural diversity can be achieved more effectively through changes in teacher attitudes, expectations, and instructional styles than through modifications to curriculum content. Factual knowledge about ethnic and cultural differences can be transmitted through the formal curriculum, as well as through school assemblies, ceremonies, and celebrations, and symbolic imagery such as school mottoes, insignia, emblems, and awards. This concept is similar in meaning to the African proverb, "It takes an entire village to raise a child." It can be modified for our purposes to read, "It takes the whole school to teach multicultural education, and every dimension of the student must be affected for it to be most effective."

Teaching the whole child also requires that the educational process be *persistent* in its culturally pluralistic commitments and actions. This is not an issue to be set apart from other educational functions, or relegated to special occasions and events. Instead, it must be a regular feature of the daily, routine operations of the educational process. Once multiculturalism becomes this pervasive in the schooling enterprise, the whole person of culturally different students is being taught through the school climate in which they live and learn, as well as through the various content and procedures used within and across the educational enterprise.

Educators must understand diverse cultures, social backgrounds, and ethnic identities, and teach *to* them as well as *through* them if they are to be successful in teaching the "whole person" of culturally diverse children. In other words, effective instructional programs employ a three-pronged approach: (1) they originate out of an understanding of how cultural traditions and experiences shape the learning potential of individuals; (2) their content and structures are determined by individual culturally different students' needs, interests, and styles; and (3) their purpose, focus, and goals are directed toward developing greater knowledge, appreciation, and acceptance of the value and vitality of cultural pluralism for all individuals. Nothing short of this unity of content, technique, intent, and context will ensure all students their incontestable educational rights as citizens of a democratic society and the human family—that is, educational equality, equity, and excellence.

Reflections and Applications

The crisis of academic achievement for students of color in the United States continues largely unabated. Despite some nominal signs of improved scores on recent standardized test measures, the long-established pattern of disproportionate academic achievement of European-Americans, Native Americans, Latinos, African-Americans, and Asian-Americans prevails. As individuals and groups of students move progressively away from being economically advantaged and Eurocentric, their performance rates plummet. And this is only one type of achievement indicator. Others, such as psychological, social, emotional, and aesthetic well-being, may be even worse. A major factor contributing to these problems is the continuing dependency of educators on one type of teaching to facilitate and assess the achievement of students who are culturally different. This practice violates virtually every principle of teaching in both general education and multicultural education.

Both general and multicultural education perspectives on the educational process emphasize principles of diversity, contextuality, developmental appropriateness, flexibility, comprehensiveness, and cultural consciousness as conditions for determining the content and quality of teaching and learning. These apply to diagnosing students' needs, selecting content and instructional strategies, providing climates for learning, and assessing learning efforts and achievement. The intentions embedded in and transmitted through these principles constitute what some educators have called "a pedagogy of and for difference" (Giroux 1992; Giroux and McLaren 1989). It means understanding the many different factors that influence how students' identities, values, and abilities are constructed, how these insights are used to develop and implement a wide variety of corresponding instructional strategies, and how goals and outcomes of education are defined to serve multiple purposes. Out of this diversity comes a new standard of educational excellence, individual self-actualization, social development, democratic citizenship, and human dignity. Cultural pluralism amplifies the interdependence and reciprocity among different ethnic, social, and racial groups, cultures, experiences, and contributions.

The other significant message to emerge from this chapter is that educational effectiveness and excellence for diverse students are contingent upon the developmental appropriateness and cultural contextuality of educational programs and practices. Because the factors that determine the learning readiness of students, the nature of scholarly truth, the equity and excellence of educational opportunities, and what is "the whole child" are multifaceted and culturally pluralistic, school programs and practices designed to respond to them must also be highly diversified. This is the only way that diverse students can be assured access to equitable opportunities so that they can achieve educational excellence. Therefore, multicultural education is a relevance and validity tool, bridge, filter, or conduit for translating general principles of teaching and learning into a framework to better understand how classroom practices can be modified to better serve the needs of students from many different racial, ethnic, social, and cultural backgrounds.

Now that you have finished reading this chapter, allow yourself some time to reflect on the ideas presented. Four activities are suggested that may help you to further clarify the principles of teaching and learning discussed in this chapter. Try some of these in your classrooms and schools with your students and colleagues.

1. Use the questions you designed at the beginning of the chapter for your *self-interview* to conduct a *post-chapter interview with yourself.* Record it. Analyze the first self-interview to see how consistent your ideas were with those discussed in the chapter. Then compare the two interviews to see if reading this chapter has caused you to modify or clarify your beliefs and assumptions about teaching and learning in culturally pluralistic settings.

2. Keep a journal of your teaching behaviors for a specified period of time, perhaps one or two weeks. In your entries, focus on what you do, when you do it, and how you "teach the whole child." At the end of the observation period, critically analyze your journal entries to determine how your instructional behaviors are distributed across the six dimensions of the human conditions suggested by Foshay, and the extent to which they are responsive to cultural diversity. If there is little cultural sensitivity, develop some ideas to modify your teaching style to correct for this. Select a few of these ideas and make a personal contract with yourself to make these changes. Include within your contract some criteria for how you will assess the quality of your change efforts.

3. Have your students read several different ethnic groups' accounts of a common event or incident. For example, they may read a female, Mexican-American, Native American, and Chinese-American interpretation of U.S. culture. Or they might interview different ethnic students, asking, "What is life like in [your school]?" Then ask your students to decide whose version is the "truth," and explain the reasons for their decisions. Explore further with the students to see how their own ethnic identities, cultural backgrounds, and other factors contribute to their decisions about what is truth.

4. Analyze the instructional materials you use as the "core resources" in your teaching to determine the degree of their ethnic and cultural

equity. To complete this task, first develop or select a set of criteria for achieving "Cultural and Ethnic Equity in Instructional Materials," based on the ideas discussed in this chapter. Additional criteria can be obtained by writing to:

> Guidelines for Selecting Bias-Free Textbooks and Storybooks
> Council on Interracial Books for Children
> P.O. Box 1263
> New York, NY 10023

> Curriculum Guidelines for MultiCultural Education (1992)
> by James A. Banks, Carlos E. Cortés, Geneva Gay, Ricardo L.
> García, and Anna Ochoa
> National Council for the Social Studies
> 3501 Newark Street, NW
> Washington, D.C. 20016

Then use your criteria to analyze instructional materials (e.g., textbooks, films and videos, literature books, test materials). Based on your findings, think of ways these materials can be improved. If no improvements are necessary, identify some specific examples of how these materials model the different elements of your criteria.

References

Asante, M. K. 1991–92. Afrocentric curriculum. *Educational Leadership* 49: 28–31.

Baker, G. C. 1983. *Planning and organizing for multicultural instruction*. Reading, Mass.: Addison-Wesley.

Banks, J. A. 1990. Citizenship education for a pluralistic democratic society. *The Social Studies* 81(5): 210–14.

Banks, J. A. 1993a. Approaches to multicultural curriculum reform. In *Multicultural education: Issues and perspectives,* ed. J. A. Banks and C. A. M. Banks, 195–214. Boston: Allyn and Bacon.

Banks, J. A. 1993b. The canon debate, knowledge construction, and multicultural education. *Educational Researcher* 22(5): 4–14.

Banks, J. A., and C. A. M. Banks, eds. 1993. *Multicultural education: Issues and perspectives*. Boston: Allyn and Bacon.

Baptiste, H. P. 1986. Multicultural education and urban schools from a sociohistorical perspective: Internalizing multiculturalism. *Journal of Educational Equity and Leadership* 6(4): 295–312.

Barbe, W. B., and R. H. Swassing. 1979. *Teaching through modality strengths: Concepts and practice.* Columbus, Ohio: Zaner-Bloser.

Bennett, C. I. 1990. *Comprehensive multicultural education: Theory and practice.* Boston: Allyn and Bacon.

Bloom, B. S., M. T. Engelhart, E. J. Furst, W. H. Hill, and R. R. Krathwohl. 1956. *Taxonomy of educational objectives, Handbook I, The cognitive domain.* New York: David McKay.

Bowers, C. A., and D. J. Flinders. 1990. *Responsive teaching: An ecological approach to classroom patterns of language, culture, and thought.* New York: Teachers College Press.

Boykin, A. W. 1986. The triple quandary and the schooling of Afro-American children. In *The school achievement of minority children: New perspectives,* ed. U. Neisser, 57–92. Hillsdale, N.J.: Lawrence Erlbaum.

Burger, H. G. 1973. Cultural pluralism and the schools. In *Cultural challenges to education: The influence of cultural factors in school learning,* ed. C. S. Brembeck and W. H. Hill. Lexington, Mass.: Lexington Books, D.C. Heath and Company.

Cazden, C. B., V. P. John., and D. Hymes. eds. 1985. *Functions of language in the classroom.* Prospect Heights, Ill.: Waveland Press.

Combs, A. W. 1991. *The schools we need: New assumptions for educational reform.* New York: Lanham.

Cone, J.H. 1984. *For my people: Black theology and the Black church.* Maryknoll, N.Y.: Orkis Books.

Darder, A. 1991. *Culture and power in the classroom: A critical foundation for bicultural education.* New York: Bergin and Garvey.

Foshay, A. W. 1975. *Essays on curriculum.* New York: Teachers College Press.

Foster, M. 1989. It's cookin' now: A performance analysis of the speech events of a black teacher in an urban community college. *Language in Society* 18(1). 1–29.

Freire, P. 1992 (1970). *Pedagogy of the oppressed.* New York: Continuum.

García, R. L. 1982. *Teaching in a pluralistic society: Concepts, models, strategies.* New York: Harper and Row.

Gay, G. 1988. Redesigning relevant curricula for diverse learners. *Education and Urban Society* 20(4). 327–40.

Gay, G. 1993. Building cultural bridges: A bold proposal for teacher education. *Education and Urban Society* 25(3): 285–99.

Gibson, M. A. 1976. Approaches to multicultural education in the United States: Some concepts and assumptions. *Anthropology and Education Quarterly* 7(4): 7–18.

Gilligan, C. 1982. *In a different voice: Psychological theory and women's development.* Cambridge, Mass.: Harvard University Press.

Giroux, H. A. 1992. *Border crossings: Cultural workers and the politics of education.* New York: Routledge.

Giroux, H. A. 1988. *Teachers as intellectuals: Toward a critical pedagogy of learning.* South Hadley, Mass.: Bergin and Garvey.

Giroux, H. A., and P. L. McLaren, eds. 1989. *Critical pedagogy, the state and cultural struggle.* Albany: State University of New York Press.

Goodlad, J. I. 1984. *A place called school: Prospects for the future*. New York: McGraw-Hill.

Greenbaum, P. E. 1985. Nonverbal differences in communication style between American Indian and Anglo elementary classrooms. *American Educational Research Journal* 22(1): 101–15.

Guthrie, J. T., and I. W. Kirsch. 1984. The emergent perspective on literacy. *Phi Delta Kappan* 65: 351–55.

Hale-Benson, J. E. 1986. *Black children: Their roots, culture, and learning styles*. Baltimore: Johns Hopkins University Press.

Halpern, D. F. 1986. *Sex differences in cognitive abilities*. Hillsdale, N.J.: Lawrence Erlbaum.

Hernandez, H. 1989. *Multicultural education: A teacher's guide to content and process*. Columbus, Ohio: Merrill.

Hilliard, A. G. 1991–92. Why we must pluralize the curriculum. *Educational Leadership* 49: 12–14.

Holliday, B. G. 1985. Towards a model of teacher-child transactional processes affecting black children's academic achievement. In *Beginnings: The social and affective development of black children,* ed. M. B. Spencer, G. K. Brookins, and W. R. Allen, 117–30. Hillsdale, N.J.: Lawrence Erlbaum.

Irvine, J. J. 1990. *Black students and school failure: Politics, practices, and prescriptions*. New York: Praeger.

King, J. E., and T. L. Wilson. 1990. Being the soul-freeing substance: A legacy of hope in Afro humanity. *Journal of Education* 172: 9–27.

Kochman, T. 1981. *Black and white styles in conflict*. Chicago: University of Chicago Press.

Ladson-Billings, G., and A. Henry. 1990. Blurring the borders: Voices of African liberatory pedagogy in the United States and Canada. *Journal of Education* 172: 72–88.

McDermott, R. 1987. Achieving school failure: An anthropological approach to illiteracy and social stratification. In *Education and cultural process: Anthropological approaches,* ed. G. D. Spindler, 173–209. Prospect Heights, Ill.: Waveland Press.

Montero-Sieburth, M. 1988. Understanding the tensions between equity and quality of secondary schooling. Journal of Educ*ation* 170(2): 122–32.

Nieto, S. 1992. A*ffirming diversity: The sociopolitical context of multicultural education.* New York: Longman.

Phenix, P. H. 1961. *Education and the common good: A moral philosophy of the curriculum*. New York: Harper and Brothers.

Phinney, J. S., and S. Traver. 1988. Ethnic identity search and commitment in black and white eighth graders. *Journal of Early Adolescence* 8: 265–77.

Ramirez, M., and A. Castañeda. 1974. *Cultural democracy, bicognitive development and education*. New York: Academic Press.

Shade, B. J., ed. 1989. *Culture, style, and the educative process*. Springfield, Ill.: Charles C. Thomas.

Shade, B. J., and C. A. New. 1993. Cultural influences on learning: Teaching implications. In *Multicultural education: Issues and perspectives*, ed. J. A. Banks and C. A. M. Banks, 317–31. Boston: Allyn and Bacon.

Shor, I. 1992. Empowering education*: Critical teaching for social change*. Chicago: The University of Chicago Press.

Sleeter, C. E., ed. 1991. *Empowerment through multicultural education*. Albany: State University of New York Press.

Sleeter, C. E., and C. A. Grant. 1988. *Making choices for multicultural education: Five approaches to race, class, and gender*. Columbus, Ohio: Merrill.

Spindler, G. D., ed. 1987. *Education and cultural process: Anthropological approaches*. Prospect Heights, Ill.: Waveland Press.

Streitmatter, J. L. 1989. Identity development and academic achievement in early adolescence. *Journal of Early Adolescence* 9: 99–116.

Suzuki, B. H. 1984. Curriculum transformation for multicultural education. *Education and Urban Society* 16: 294–322.

Taba, H. 1962. *Curriculum development: Theory and practice*. New York: Harcourt, Brace and World.

Thorpe, L. P., and A. M. Schmuller. 1954. *Contemporary theories of learning with applications to education and psychology*. New York: The Ronald Press.

Epilogue

It seems appropriate to end this book the way it began, by placing multicultural education in the philosophical context and perspective of general education values and beliefs. Despite the claims of some critics, multicultural education is not un-American or antidemocratic. It is not the dream of irrational extremists bent on destroying the unity of the country and its European-based cultural heritages. Nor is it a set of irresponsible and unsound pedagogical suggestions that reduce education to merely making ethnic minorities feel good about themselves. Quite the contrary.

Multicultural education is the birthchild of Western ideals about civic and educational freedom, equality, justice, dignity, and excellence. It was initially conceived in the civil rights movement of the late 1960s with its emphasis on removing legal restrictions to the rights and opportunities of individuals from ethnic and racial groups who have been victims of oppression and exploitation in U.S. society and schools. Civic leaders' efforts in political and social arenas to extend full rights to all citizens of the nation parallel multicultural education proponents' efforts in schools. In effect, their mission is to use democratic imperatives as the ideological foundation for changing schooling, making its structure, content, processes, and practices more egalitarian, representative, and effective for all children. Thus, in ideology, content, methodology, intent, and essence, multicultural education is fundamentally an attempt to democratize the educational enterprise.

It is also a very humanistic and progressive enterprise. Like many educational innovations that preceded it and others that operate in tandem with it, multicultural education gains its momentum and vision from ethical, moral, and pedagogical principles deeply ingrained in the fabric of Western social, political, and educational thought. It gives preeminence to the child as the center of all educational decision making; it extends the concepts of freedom, equality, and justice to policies, programs, and practices in schools; it facilitates the personal empowerment and self-actualization of students by affirming their personal and cultural identities; it maximizes students' academic achievement and enhances their developing sociopolitical action skills; it helps students acquire the knowledge, attitudes, and values needed to improve the quality of individual and communal lives.

As demographics change, reflecting the changes in the ethnic and cultural diversity of society, the United States is shown to be evolving toward becoming a microcosm of the global society. Many of the dynamics that justify the need for multicultural education are similar to those that undergird global education, such as growing economic interdependence among culturally different peoples, tension between cultural democracy and cultural imperialism, violation of civic and human rights, unequal distribution of rights, privileges, resources, and political power, and the civil right to high-quality education for everyone. For these reasons, many proponents of multicultural education suggest that it establishes a foundation from which students and teachers can build citizenship skills for the global village.

Another central theme in multicultural education is the idea that an interactive, reciprocal relationship exists between the intellectual growth of individuals and the economic and social development of society. The preeminent responsibility of educational institutions is to serve the needs of their individual clients and the social systems in which they function. A salient and undeniable characteristic of these two constituencies in the United States is pluralism—racial, ethnic, cultural, and social. Of necessity then, to be adequate—not to mention to aspire toward excellence—and to fulfill its most basic functions, education in this country must be multicultural. Within this context, transmitting the heritage and collective knowledge of the culture, and socializing youth into their roles, rights, and responsibilities, are functions that require the inclusion of cultural pluralism in the educational process. This is necessary in order to achieve educational quality, relevance, representation, and excellence for all students.

There is very little mystery about multicultural education. It is simply an effort to improve the quality of education provided for all students in all societies. It advocates that *all* children, including the poor and the middle class, African-Americans, Native Americans, Latinos, Asian-Americans and European-Americans, males and females, English and non-English speakers, recently arrived immigrants and indigenous groups, deserve the very best education that the nation can provide—now and in the future. This is both a human and a democratic citizenship right. Since education is always filtered through cultural screens, and since the United States is a culturally pluralistic society, all decisions about the content, process, and context of teaching and learning must be multicultural.

It is a fact that culture has a determining influence on all aspects of human life, including teaching and learning. Because students and teachers come from many different cultural backgrounds, school practices, if they are to be based on ethical and pedagogical standards of good teaching, such as readiness, scholarly truth, relevance, validity, developmental appropriateness, and teaching the whole child, must be culturally pluralistic. Anything less, in a significantly and increasingly diverse society like the United States, leads to unnecessarily strident practices of cultural imposition, discrimination, and hegemony. Consequently, national ideals of achieving universal literacy, respecting individual differences, and creating educational excellence for everyone are unattainable without a companion commitment to cultural and ethnic equity. Excellence and equity are so closely interwoven and dialectically related that one cannot be achieved without simultaneously attending to the other.

Therefore, multicultural education is, at its essence, a way to conceptualize and translate principles of good pedagogy, commonly accepted theories of learning, and conceptions of education for democratic citizenship into programs and practices that are appropriate for the social, political, cultural, ethnic, and racial realities of the United States. Its value commitment, targets of change, and intended outcomes are informed by the same libertarian and democratic principles that govern general education. Both aim to create better individuals and improve society by making cultural legacies, cultural capital, and individual potential readily accessible to and feasible for everyone. The only difference is that multicultural education recognizes and celebrates specific cultural and ethnic segments of the population, while general education conceives of students in more global and universal terms. The relationship between these two conceptions of teaching and learning is very complementary. It is similar to other classic relationships, such as those that exist between theory and practice, general and specific, local and universal, means and ends, ideals and realities. Both are necessary to make education successful for our culturally pluralistic students and society.

All strategies that expedite the achievement of these goals should be enthusiastically welcomed by educators and the general public alike. Despite

Epilogue

the controversy, confusion, and misconceptions that surround it, multicultural education has the potential to improve the quality of educational opportunities and outcomes for *all* students and to better prepare them to become active agents of social change, committed to reforming society so that it is more free, equal, and just for ethnically and culturally diverse individuals and groups. To speak separately of multicultural education and good education is rapidly becoming redundant. Within the United States and the world, education that reflects existing realities and is designed to prepare students for the projected future must be multicultural. Education that is not multicultural retards the possibility of both society and individuals reaching their maximal potential on all levels—intellectually, socially, politically, economically, morally, ethically, and aesthetically.

Index

Note: page numbers in **boldface** indicate a chart, diagram, or figure.

Index

developmental appropriateness, 130–39

developmental tasks, 69–74

Dewey, John, influence of, 63, 92, 95

discrimination, assumptions about, 127

dissent, right of, 102

Disuniting of America, The (Schlesinger), 37

developmental psychology, 63–88

developmental stages, variability of, 66

diversity, M. Angelou on, 1; and democratic principles, 20–21; as definitive human trait, 107–8; increasing, 1–2, 109–10; and values of unity, 33–34, 36–38; versus majority rule, 96–97

E

education, as basic right, 96–100; defined (Hitt), 17–18; empowering (Shor), 16–17; as foundation of democracy, 19–20; for freedom, 45–46; functions of, 4, 16; for racial equality, 106–7; same versus equal, 35; social service goals of, 91–92

Education and the Common Good (Phenix), 92–96

educational principles, 4; as bridge between general and multicultural education, 55–56; categories of, 16–26; and change, 25–26; for citizenship and socialization, 18–22, **22;** general, 11–29; general compared to multicultural, 7; for human development, 16–18, **19;** multicultural translations of, 46–54, **47;** from professional literature, 15–16; role of, 12; sources of, 12–16; suggested by survey of educators, 14–15; for teaching and learning, 23–26, **24–25**

educational reform, 27; and lag between theory and practice, 43; multicultural education as, 34–35

educators, and educational principles, 14–15

ego identity, 77

empowering education, 16–17

equity, concept of, 126–27; and excellence, 126–29; meaning of, 127

equivalency of effect potential, 128

Erikson's Crisis Theory of Personality Development, 75–77, **76,** 78

ethical values, and democracy, 101–2

ethnic enclaves, 104

ethnic identity, 78-79; and learning readiness, 133

ethnic literacy, as contextual factor, 121–22

ethnic particularism (Ravitch), 37–38

ethnocentrism, 79; due to lack of information, 121

Eurocentrism, and cultural variations in development, 67

excellence, and equity, 126–29; meaning of, 127

"expanding spiral" curriculum, 71

F

fraternity, and democracy, 102–3

freedom, education for, 45–46

G

gang wannabe behavior, 73, 74

gender, and learning style, 138

gender liberation movement, 101

general education, principles of, 11–29. *See also* **educational principles**

gestalt **approach,** 71–72

global interdependence, 99

Guidelines for Selecting Bias-Free Textbooks and Storybooks, 144–45

H

"hanging on the wall," 53

heredity, and environment interaction, 64

holistic education, 139-42

holistic growth, 65–69

homogeneity, assumption of, 127

human(s), dual nature of, 17–18

human condition, dimensions of, 140

human development, basic principles of, 86; dualism in, 17–18; as educational function, 16–18; and general educational principles, **19;** holistic growth, 65–69; and the humane person, 18; and learning complexity, 131; principles of, 63–88; roles of heredity and environment, 64; theoretical concepts, 64; variability in changes, 67–68

"humane" person, 18

I

identity development, 74–79; dimensions of, 74

Illiberal Education (D'Souza), 38

individual development. *See* **human development**

individual differences, 80–85; and equal treatment, 85; and human development, 69; and learning, 23; and national culture, 42

individualism, and capitalism, 21–22

individuality, and universality, 80–85

instructional variability, 80

intellectual process, multicultural application of, 121–22

intelligence, contextual nature of, 81–82; defined (Gardner), 80–82; logical-mathematical, 81; types of, 80–82

interpersonal relations, and desegregation, 104–5

Index

Reflections and Applications

Reflections and Applications

Reflections and Applications

Reflections and Applications